WASHINGTON
WINE + FOOD
THE COOKBOOK

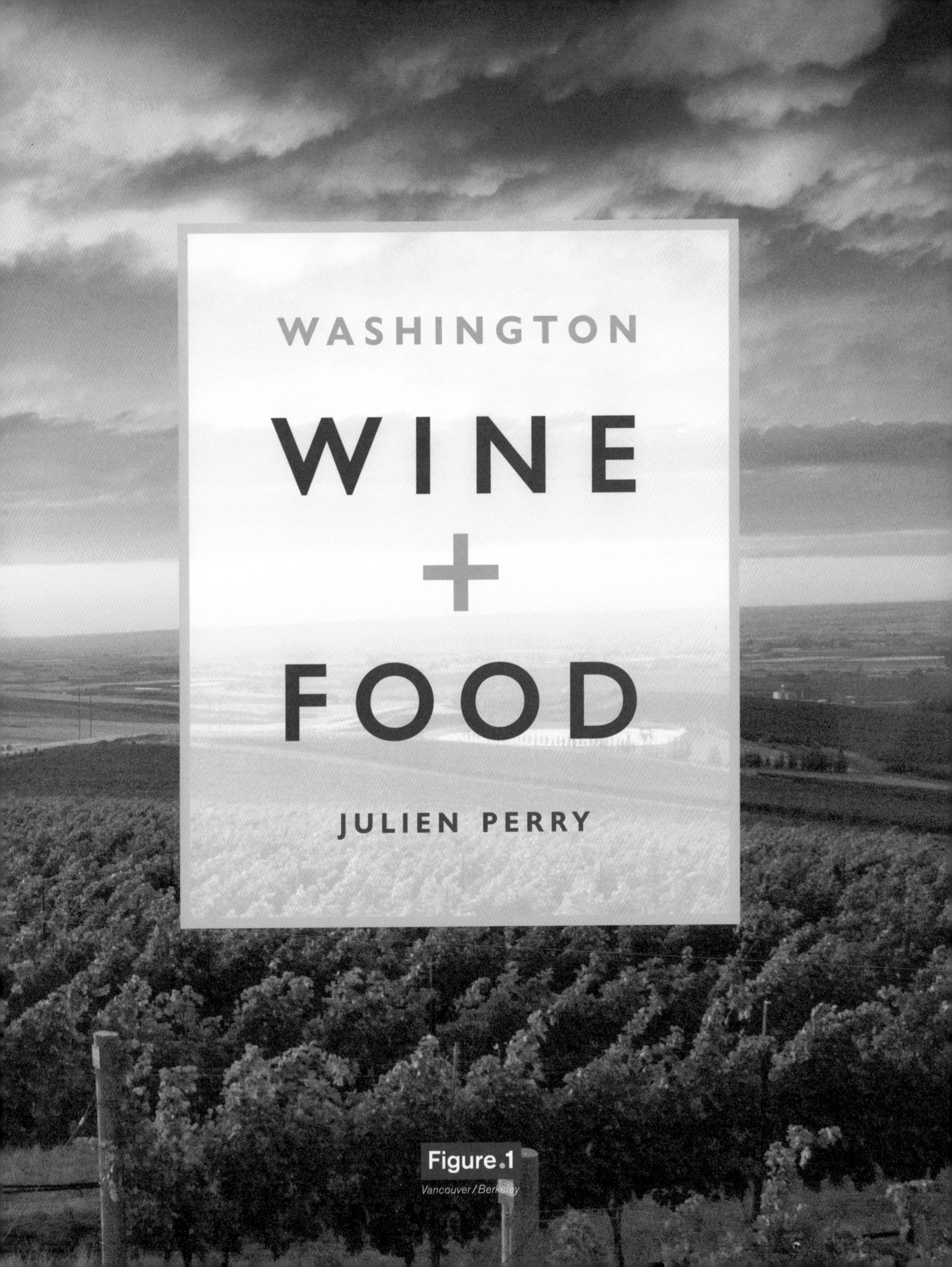

WASHINGTON
WINE
+
FOOD

JULIEN PERRY

Figure.1

Vancouver / Berkeley

TO THOSE WHO APPRECIATE THE THRILL OF OPENING A BOTTLE OF WINE, THE MAGIC THAT HAPPENS WHILE CONSUMING IT, AND THE PASSION THAT GOES INTO MAKING IT.

Cataloguing data is available from Library and Archives Canada
ISBN 978-1-77327-104-0 (hbk.)

Design by Jessica Sullivan
All photography by Charity Burggraaf,
except pages 2–3, 20–21, 32, 66, 71, 167, 186, 197, 202, 222
courtesy of Washington State Wine/Andrea Johnson Photography
Food styling by Nathan Carrabba
Map reference courtesy of Washington State Wine

Editing by Michelle Meade
Copy editing by Grace Yaginuma
Proofreading by Renate Preuss
Indexing by Gillian Watts

Printed and bound in China by C&C Offset Printing Co., Ltd.
Distributed internationally by Publishers Group West

Figure 1 Publishing Inc.
Vancouver BC Canada
www.figure1publishing.com

RECIPE NOTES:
All herbs are fresh unless stated otherwise.

Butter is unsalted unless stated otherwise.

Eggs are large unless stated otherwise.

Produce is always medium-sized unless stated otherwise.

Citrus juices are freshly squeezed.

CONTENTS

FOREWORD

I'm from Yakima, on the east side of Washington state. I grew up on Avalanche Avenue with my brothers, Craig and Kent, and my parents, Kent and Cathy. My dad loved his garden, and my brothers and I spent countless hours working beside him. He cared for huge beds of flowers and an abundant vegetable garden in our backyard. The fruit trees such as Bartlett pears and Golden Delicious, Winesap, and Pippin apples had become lonely sentinels from the orchard that had been there before houses. My dad had a green thumb, maybe more like a green arm, because *everything* he touched, thrived.

My brothers and I would frequently travel with our dad to the Lower Valley during the summer, visiting farm stands up and down Lateral A Road in Wapato, buying produce from local farmers. During late summer and fall harvests, my brothers and I spent weekends alongside my mom and grandmother canning pears, peaches, and cherries in the Lower Valley. One brother would halve the peaches, another would fill the can with a cup of sugar, and the third would stamp the bottom of the can with an inked number.

Farm-to-table was how I grew up and fresh fruit and vegetables were at the forefront of the dining table. Not that my brothers and I appreciated the bounty of the Yakima Valley at the time! It took adulthood to understand how special this life in this valley really was, which partially explains why I returned in 2005 to Eastern Washington. I came home to spend more time with my dad and my brothers, coupled with a curiosity about this new business I was hearing about... *wine*. I wanted to be part of it and find a way to turn this curiosity into something tangible. I wanted to make wine from the same region where I'd grown up.

With its tortured scablands and dry rocky plateaus, Eastern Washington is an acquired taste and can be hard to love, unless you're from here. Vineyards take root in unforgiving soils deposited over thousands of years by a series of cataclysmic mega-floods. Climate, geography, and geology combine here to create wines with an alluring mix of Old World elegance and New World grandeur.

My interest in wine began in the mid-eighties. After moving to L.A. to pursue my acting career, I frequently returned to Yakima to visit my father. Together, we would explore the burgeoning wine scene—Yakima was Washington's first AVA, created back in 1983, and now the state is the second biggest producer of wine in America, after California. Later, inspired by friends in Napa Valley, the notion of making my own wine took hold. A Washington wine would allow me to see family more often, I reasoned, and the Washington Cabernet Sauvignons and Syrahs I tasted were spectacular. A chance meeting with Walla Walla winemaker Eric Dunham led to the simple handshake that launched Pursued by Bear in 2005. A friend suggested the name, inspired by Shakespeare's most famous stage direction, "Exit, pursued by a bear," from *The Winter's Tale*. In 2008, Eric passed the winemaking baton to Daniel Wampfler (page 22), who crafts our wines with the same care that Eric inspired. We make limited amounts of Cabernet Sauvignon, Syrah, and rosé that taste like Yakima: beautiful, brambly dark fruits, blackberry, plum, cherry, earthiness, and minerality, with a structure that wraps around you. And always that bright freshness, which comes from the blazing hot days and cool nights, and makes people realize the impending greatness of Washington state.

I love walking the vineyards in the weeks leading up to harvest. I love getting my hands purple with grape juice during crush. And I love the fact that wine has brought me home. I feel a little bit like I'm a self-appointed ambassador of my home state's wines. I'm proud of the state's growers and vintners who have brought Washington wines to the world stage.

My Pursued by Bear journey has been exciting and revealing, rewarding and challenging, and it could not have happened were it not for the exceptional people who work in all areas of this wonderful Washington state industry. I am one small piece of this industry that has given me so much.

Each winemaker and winery owner in this book tells a different story about their journey into the world of Washington wine. Stories as diverse as the grape varieties that can be grown successfully in this great state. We all share the passion of conviction that world-class wine is being made here. We recognize that we share this journey and realize we are telling the story of Washington wine with many voices and as one song.

KYLE MACLACHLAN
Owner and vintner of Pursued by Bear

INTRODUCTION

It's not just about what's in the bottle. There is a cultural element to what makes Washington wine great. And beyond the bounty of grapes is a gritty Northwest spirit that's experimental in nature. There's arguably never been a better time to be a winemaker in Washington, or even a wine drinker.

Talking to the winemakers in this book, it was immediately apparent that winemaking requires a lot of passion, tenacity, and hard work for a desired result that, just like art, may or may not appeal to the masses. It's a personal pursuit that's neither for the faint of heart nor the apathetic; one needs determination and a willingness to endure hours of intense physical labor for, oftentimes, modest financial gain. But even when acknowledging the many hardships of a craft that called to them, Washington winemakers forge ahead with palpable joy and sincerity. And how could they not? Each of these winemakers fell in love with an industry in a state that produces some of the best grapes on the planet.

People outside of Washington often assume the weather and climate to be one big wet and rainy mess. While that may be true for some parts of the state, many regions—the ones that excel at growing grapes—are exempt from this tired trope. Despite being an ocean apart, Walla Walla has similar grape-growing conditions to Bordeaux and Burgundy because they share a similar latitude (which governs the length of day and the angle of the sun), making both ideal locations for wine production.

What makes Washington an ideal grape-growing region? Climate, geography, and geology. The combination produces wines that bridge the New World and Old World—two terms often mentioned in this book. Old World refers to lighter-bodied wines coming from stalwart wine regions such as France and Italy. New World is the exact opposite. These bolder and more experimental wines originate from non-traditional winemaking regions, like California and Australia. The combination of the two makes Washington wines distinct.

We are a young industry by winemaking standards (we're just barely a twinkle in the eyes of Italy and France), yet Washington is the second-largest wine producer in the country, just behind California, with more than a thousand wineries and counting. Vintners settled in Washington state for the same reason Boeing, Starbucks, Microsoft, Amazon, and other big

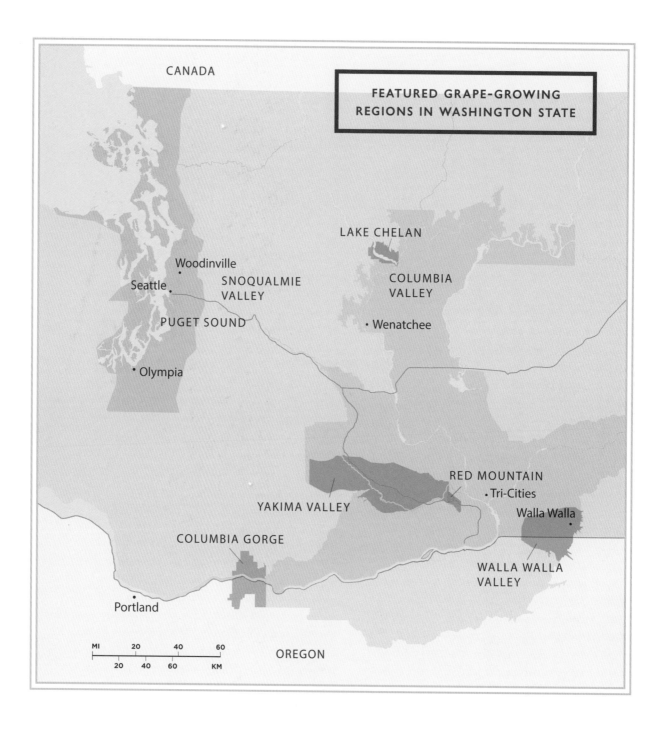

FEATURED GRAPE-GROWING
REGIONS IN WASHINGTON STATE

CANADA

LAKE CHELAN

COLUMBIA
VALLEY

Woodinville
Seattle
SNOQUALMIE
VALLEY

PUGET SOUND

• Wenatchee

• Olympia

RED MOUNTAIN
• Tri-Cities

YAKIMA VALLEY

Walla Walla

COLUMBIA GORGE

WALLA WALLA
VALLEY

Portland

MI   20   40   60
   20 40 60   KM

OREGON

companies started here: there's a shared vigor that seeds innovation, adventure, and an ambition for greatness. And that sense of wonder catalyzed some of our state's key wine regions. For example, John Williams and Jim Holmes, who first established Red Mountain (page 136), were connected to the engineering research that took place at Hanford in the 1960s—they were intellectually inclined and scientifically minded enough to see the potential of a great grape-growing region in the middle of the sagebrush.

Walla Walla has a longer history punctuated by the influence of people choosing to relocate to an area with rich soil, a grape-friendly climate, and a strong sense of community. This popular wine destination was built on the passion of the people who reside there. Pop open a bottle of wine made with grapes from either region and you'll be able to taste the thread that connects the two.

Fruit quality is the common ground between all of Washington's wine regions, but while the state grows incredible grapes, there are significant differences characterized by their locality.

GRAPE-GROWING REGIONS

Nearly all of Washington's wine comes from grapes grown east of the Cascade Mountains in the Columbia Valley, which was carved out by the Missoula floods during the Ice Age, which in turn created perfect soils for grape growing. At more than fifty-five thousand acres, this stretch of land is larger than Napa!

There are currently fourteen American Viticultural Areas (AVA) in Washington state, and this book highlights some of the major ones.

Red Mountain In the southeast corner of the state, Red Mountain produces grapes that are powerful and intense—both in flavor and color—because the hotter, drier climate allows them to ripen more easily, which produces a higher sugar content. Cabernet Sauvignon is king on Red Mountain, along with the majority of our full-bodied, fruit-forward red wines.

Yakima Valley The first AVA established in Washington in 1983, Yakima Valley contains over a third of the state's vineyards and encompasses three sub-AVAs: Red Mountain, Snipes Mountain, and Rattlesnake Hills. Its diverse climate produces both warm-weather and cooler-climate grapes. Over half of Washington's Chardonnay and Riesling comes from Yakima Valley, which also yields a significant amount of the state's best Merlot, Syrah, and Cabernet Sauvignon.

Walla Walla About two hours east of Yakima Valley, in the foothills of the Blue Mountains, Walla Walla gets measurably more rainfall than Red Mountain. While both regions produce similar wines (Cabernet Sauvignon, Syrah), Walla Walla valley wines tend to be a little more restrained.

Lake Chelan Farther north, nestled along the slope of a fifty-mile-long lake, the milder temperatures of Lake Chelan also create a favorable climate for grape growing. And because of the Ice Age glaciers that forged it, the soil is rich in minerals and nutrients, thus creating fruit that exhibits the same characteristics. Malbec, Pinot Noir, Riesling, and Gewürztraminer grapes do particularly well here.

Columbia Gorge Grapes grown in the region straddling the Washington and Oregon border, in the rain shadow of the Cascade Mountains, produce cool-climate reds, such as Cabernet Franc, and stunning whites including Chardonnay, Riesling, Grüner Veltliner, and Gewürztraminer. In fact, the Gorge is one of the few regions in Washington that produces more white wines than red.

Because of these unique regional characteristics, there is a greater bipartition of the wine industry between growing and winemaking. Winemakers here are able to source their fruit from whatever region they'd like, regardless of where their winery is located. It's also not uncommon for winemakers who own their own vineyards—such as Cairdeas (page 54), Va Piano (page 210), and Pepper Bridge (page 28)—to supplement their fruit from other parts of the state; Washington winemakers have an expansive playground to experiment with, unrestricted by geography.

GRAPE VARIETIES

According to the Washington State Wine Commission, Washington produces nearly seventy wine-grape varieties with about 59 percent of those being red. As it's still a young wine country, we may continue to see the introduction of more grape varieties in the region because of our vast microclimates.

RED GRAPES

Our most common red grape varieties include Cabernet Sauvignon, Merlot, and Syrah, but Cabernet Franc, Pinot Noir, Malbec, and Grenache can also be grown.

Cabernet Sauvignon As one of the world's most commonly grown red wine grape varieties, Cabernet Sauvignon grows in abundance in Washington. It is fruity with notes of black currant, cherry, berry, chocolate, leather, herbs, or even a combination of them all. Moreover, it can develop a beautiful body over an extended time period (about several years of bottle aging). Many vintners will exercise traditional practices by adding Merlot or Cab Franc (*see also* Bordeaux-style wines, page 14). It can be served with red meat (burgers and steaks come to mind!), cheeseboards, and even grilled portobello mushrooms.

Merlot It means "little blackbird" in French, and this classic, approachable wine is known for being rounded and brimming with cherry notes and complex aromas such as mint, cigar box, and spices like nutmeg and cardamom. As they have the tendency to be moderately tannic with slightly greater alcohol content and higher acidity than other wines, Merlots were traditionally used in blends. Today, the wine has gained popularity in its own right. Pair it with tomato-based dishes as well as those with deep umami flavors, including roast chicken, mushrooms, and Parmesan.

Syrah Also known as Shiraz in Australia, this dark-skinned red grape variety has ruled over the Northern Rhône Valley in France for centuries and is a relative newcomer to Washington state. Known as a spicy, rich, complex varietal, Syrah boasts luscious aromas and flavors including blackberries, black currants, roasted coffee, and leather. It is often recommended for all types of roast, grilled, or smoked meats.

WASHINGTON WINES: FACT SHEET

National rank: 2nd-largest premium wine producer in the United States

Number of wineries: 970+

Number of wine-grape growers: 350+

Varieties produced: 70+

Wine production: Approximately 17.5 million cases

Average hours of summer sunlight: 16 hours per day (an extra hour more than California's prime growing region)

Annual rainfall: 6 to 8 inches in eastern Washington (the major grape-growing region); 35 to 38 inches in western Washington

HARVESTED IN 2018: 261,000 TONS

59% RED = 153,400 TONS

41% WHITE = 107,600 TONS

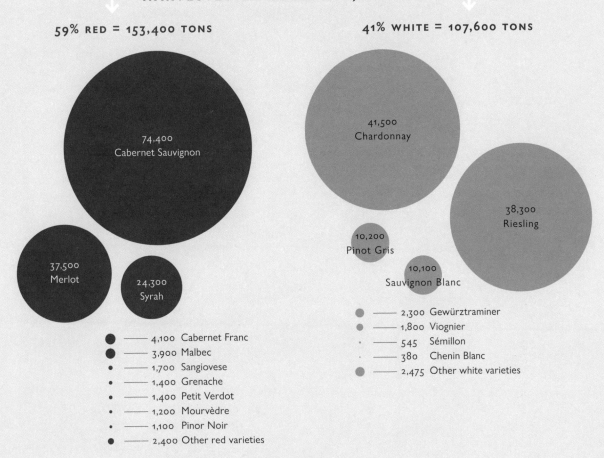

74,400 Cabernet Sauvignon

37,500 Merlot

24,300 Syrah

41,500 Chardonnay

38,300 Riesling

10,200 Pinot Gris

10,100 Sauvignon Blanc

- 4,100 Cabernet Franc
- 3,900 Malbec
- 1,700 Sangiovese
- 1,400 Grenache
- 1,400 Petit Verdot
- 1,200 Mourvèdre
- 1,100 Pinor Noir
- 2,400 Other red varieties

- 2,300 Gewürztraminer
- 1,800 Viognier
- 545 Sémillon
- 380 Chenin Blanc
- 2,475 Other white varieties

NUMBER OF WINERIES IN WASHINGTON

2018	2017	2016	2015	2014	2013	2012	2011	2010	2009
970	940	900+	890+	871	818	760	740	686	620

At times, Washington makers will produce Bordeaux-style wines, which is reference to a wine style and not necessarily a specific grape. Bordeaux-style red wines are blended of Cabernet Sauvignon, Merlot, Cabernet Franc, Malbec, and Petite Verdot grapes. Similarly, Rhône-style wines are styled in the wines of France's Rhône Valley. Traditionally, these blends are made with Grenache and have elevated alcohol levels and beautiful ripe fruit to create rounded, warm, red fruit flavors.

WHITE GRAPES

While the majority of wine production favors just a few white varieties (Chardonnay and Riesling alone make up about 80 percent of Washington's annual white wine grape harvest), the state also grows, and is starting to experiment more with, less familiar grapes such as Sémillon, Viognier, Picpoul, Chenin Blanc, Grenache Blanc, Roussanne, and Grüner Veltliner. More winemakers are seeking out these cooler-climate grapes in order to add diversity to Washington's red-heavy tasting landscape.

Chardonnay Grown in Washington since the 1960s, Chardonnay is one of the most popular white grape varieties in the region. While Chardonnays from other regions tend to be rich and powerful, Washington Chardonnays have a crisp and delicate note with subtle oakiness to accentuate the varietal's character. Serve them with lighter dishes such as steamed or grilled fish, seafood, pasta or risotto with spring vegetables, or salads.

Riesling Washington is the country's largest producing region of Riesling—and for good reason. The Columbia Valley's high summer temperatures and cool evenings create full-flavored wines, often with floral notes and bright peach, apricot, and apple notes. Because Rieslings are so well-balanced between acidity and sugar, they can be paired with lighter fare as well as rich dishes with hearty sauces. And for those wine lovers who enjoy wines on the sweeter side, a Riesling makes an ideal choice to ground the heat of spicier foods.

Sauvignon Blanc These wines have distinctive fruity and herbaceous flavors, depending on the climate. Crisp, elegant, and fresh, they are best paired with fish, seafood, or cheese such as chèvre. They are also one of the few wines to complement sushi.

Gewürztraminer This aromatic wine grape variety has an intense floral bouquet with hints of allspice and tropical fruits. Drier styles pair nicely with spicy food and can even be substituted for rich reds.

WHAT GROWS TOGETHER, GOES TOGETHER

I'd be remiss not to talk about why Washington grapes are the perfect companion for food. Washington wines have a natural acidity which makes them inherently food friendly. The grapes have an intense but short ripening period (generally April through October) that is characterized by the shift from warm days to cool nights. When it's hot, grapes ripen up and develop those big, beautiful flavors, while the drop in temperature allows them to retain the acidity that has accumulated all day.

In fact, Washington has some of the most dramatic fluctuations of any wine region in the world, and this phenomenon—known as the diurnal shift—is one of the greatest natural resources for growing grapes. Because of the dramatic temperature swings, the fruit ends up balanced between ripe sugars (which equates to alcohol in the wine) and crisp acidity.

There's a common expression amongst chefs and wine lovers: "What grows together, goes together." It's why crisp Washington Chardonnays pair so well with apples such as Gala, Fuji, and Cameo. And while you likely associate our big Cabernets and Syrahs with powerhouse flavor bombs, there's also an underlying earthiness and minerality to them that makes them so favorably matched with red meat, mushrooms and other woodsy, foraged vegetables that have become signature Washington ingredients.

There are nearly sixty thousand acres of vineyards in Washington state being utilized for wine, and that's only about a quarter of the land that's available. Not only is there a seemingly endless variety of excellent fruit to coax wine from, but the growth potential is off the charts.

Passionate winemakers are ubiquitous throughout the world, but in Washington, winemakers just like making delicious wine. As I discovered throughout the process of writing this book, they're not trying to create the next Bordeaux or Napa; they simply want to honor and realize the potential of local grapes. Before Washington ever became popular for wine production, it was mainly farmland. And

winemakers here want to retain and sustain that organic relationship-based sense of place, community, and camaraderie.

The same "wild west" Pacific Northwest spirit found among this propulsive community has also enabled a cadre of talented chefs to flourish here. Great hospitality is presented in an approachable manner—we may not have a lot of white tablecloths in Washington state, but we still have a killer fine-dining scene. That same quality extends to our winemakers: our standard go-to uniform includes Carhartt and Muck boots, but we produce some of the best wines in the world.

This book is a celebration of winemakers who have helped to define Washington's flourishing wine scene. In addition, some of the best chefs from Seattle have created recipes to complement the signature wines from these talented craftspeople, many of which feature native ingredients—such as stinging nettles, Skagit Valley strawberries, and local shellfish—that truly celebrate the community, food, and wine culture here in Washington state.

With a bountiful selection of the best Washington wines and ingredients at your fingertips, I'm hopeful you will be inspired to create a meal inclusive of both. I'm equally encouraged that you'll want to explore local wines and wineries after reading the backstories of these vintners, these community members who have put in tireless hours to create products that they're proud of and that you'll hopefully enjoy. Now, go find the corkscrew and get ready to drink it all in!

THE WINERIES

THE RECIPES

WASHINGTON

WINE

+

FOOD

THE COOKBOOK

ABEJA

+

DAN WAMPFLER AND AMY ALVAREZ-WAMPFLER

One of Walla Walla's most bucolic destinations is a beautiful pastoral inn situated on a forty-acre, century-old restored farmstead in the Blue Mountains. But Abeja (meaning "bee" in Spanish) has new winemakers who are living their own utopia.

Dan Wampfler and his wife, Amy, who also worked together at Columbia Crest (Amy made the whites, Dan the reds), have been making wine collectively for more than thirty years. The couple moved to Walla Walla in 2008 when Dan was hired as head winemaker for Dunham Cellars. Two years later, Amy was hired as head winemaker of Sinclair Estate Vineyards.

In 2016, they were both offered the opportunity to join Abeja, taking over the winemaking duties from John Abbott, who helped founders Ken and Ginger Harrison launch the winery back in the early 2000s. "Amy and I met through our passion for winemaking," says Dan. "Our dream was to make wine together from start to finish with one label under one roof."

The balanced, age-worthy wines are estate driven, respectful of vintage, and aligned with Dan and Amy's style. And even though Abeja is known as a Cab Sauv house, they have been recognized for their Chardonnay, Viognier, and Cab Franc. "We bring romance to the wines, but the quality has been consistent from the inception of the winery," Dan shares. "Abeja is so much more than a wine and food experience—it's an enchanting, all-encompassing place. We feel as though we've won the winemaking lottery."

> *Chestnut Pappardelle with Corn and Chanterelle "Sugo"* | *p. 24*

CHESTNUT PAPPARDELLE
with Corn and Chanterelle "Sugo"

CHEF: QUINTON STEWART, BEN PARIS

Pictured p. 23

SERVES 4 TO 6

WINE PAIRING: Abeja Cabernet Sauvignon

This satisfying and flavorful vegetarian pasta dish can be adapted with seasonal ingredients: fava beans in the spring, English peas in the summer, or roasted squash in the fall. The Cabernet Sauvignon stands up to the buttery sauce: its rich dark fruit and cacao notes complement the sweet corn and earthy flavors of the mushrooms and the chestnut pasta.

MUSHROOM STOCK In a saucepan, combine mushrooms, shallot, and thyme. Add 2 quarts of water and bring to a gentle simmer. Cook for 1 hour, uncovered. Strain through a cheesecloth and reserve until needed.

CHESTNUT PAPPARDELLE In a stand mixer fitted with a hook attachment, combine all ingredients and knead on low speed for 3 to 4 minutes, until a smooth and shiny dough forms. (If it doesn't come together, add a few drops of water.) Wrap it tightly in plastic wrap and rest for 20 minutes.

Pass the dough through a pasta machine 4 to 5 times, starting on setting #10 and working your way down to #2. (When you can see your hand through the pasta sheet, it's thin enough to cook with.) Cut it into ¾-inch-wide noodles. Dredge pappardelle in semolina to prevent them from sticking together. Divide the pasta in half, then store one half for future use (see Note).

MUSHROOM STOCK
2 lbs cremini mushrooms, thinly sliced
5 large shallots, thinly sliced
4 sprigs thyme

CHESTNUT PAPPARDELLE
4 cups all-purpose flour
2 cups chestnut flour
1 cup semolina flour, plus extra for dredging
7 eggs
Pinch of salt
1 tsp good-quality olive oil

NOTE: The recipe makes more than double the amount of pasta dough required for the dish, but you can freeze the uncooked pappardelle. When ready to use, simply cook from frozen (do not defrost) and add an extra 30 seconds to the cooking time.

Bring a stockpot of salted water to a boil. Separate pappardelle, add it to the pot, and cook for 3 to 4 minutes, until just al dente. Drain and set aside.

CHANTERELLE "SUGO" Melt 2 tablespoons butter in a large skillet over medium-high heat until it begins to brown. Add chanterelles, working in batches if necessary to avoid overcrowding. (If working in batches, divide butter accordingly.) Cook for 2 to 3 minutes, untouched, to caramelize. Toss to brown on all sides. Add a good pinch of salt, shallot, garlic, corn, and thyme. Remove from heat and deglaze with wine. Add stock and 2 tablespoons butter and bring to a simmer.

ASSEMBLY Add pappardelle to the pan and fold in. Simmer for another 1 to 2 minutes, until sauce is thick enough to coat the pasta. Add parsley and a squeeze of lemon. Season to taste with salt and pepper.

Transfer pasta to a large serving platter or individual bowls and sprinkle pecorino on top. Serve immediately.

SEARED SCALLOPS IN HERB STOCK with Calamari
and Savory Clams CHEF: QUINTON STEWART, BEN PARIS

WINE PAIRING: Abeja Chardonnay

This elegant coastal recipe is the perfect expression of our Pacific coast, speaking to the bounty of seafood that comes our way. If scallops and clams are unavailable, try seared halibut or cod—they make a great centerpiece—with mussels as a supporting act. No matter what you decide, just be sure to serve it with crusty baguette.

The sweet, briny shellfish and the broth need a good wine with acidity and body. Abeja's Chardonnay, with its bouquet of mandarin and lemon verbena, brings a beautiful and complex aroma to the pairing.

SALSA VERDE Add all ingredients except the oil and salt and pepper to a food processor or a blender. Process on low speed, gradually adding enough oil to make a loose paste. Season with salt and pepper. Set aside. (Leftover salsa verde can be stored in the refrigerator for up to 2 weeks. It can be served with pork, lamb, beef, salmon, or shrimp.)

HERB STOCK Melt butter in a stockpot over medium heat. Add onion, carrots, and celery and sauté for 3 to 5 minutes, until fragrant. Add fish bones, clams, and wine, cover, reduce heat to low, and cook for another 3 to 4 minutes. Add 2 quarts water, garlic, bay leaves, and parsley stems. Bring to a boil, remove from heat, and set aside, covered, for 20 minutes. Season with salt to taste. Strain stock through a cheesecloth, discard clams, and set aside. (Leftover stock can be stored in airtight containers in the freezer for up to 3 months.)

SALSA VERDE
10 green olives, pitted
6 anchovy fillets
3 cloves garlic
1 jalapeño, deseeded and deveined
¼ cup oregano leaves
Bunch of parsley, leaves only (reserve stems for the stock)
Bunch of mint, leaves only
Grated zest of 1 lemon
Good-quality olive oil
Salt and black pepper, to taste

HERB STOCK
¼ cup (½ stick) butter
1 small onion, finely chopped
2 carrots, finely chopped
2 stalks celery, finely chopped
3 lbs fish bones (any white fish, such as halibut or cod)
1 lb clams, cleaned
1 cup white wine
2 cloves garlic
2 bay leaves
Reserved parsley stems
Salt

3 Tbsp + ¼ cup olive oil (divided),
  plus extra if needed
1 lb clams, cleaned
½ lb squid, cleaned and cut into
  bite-sized pieces
2 cups Seafood Stock (see here)
2 Tbsp butter
Juice of 1 lemon (divided)
Sea salt, to taste
6 large sea scallops
3 Tbsp Salsa Verde (see here)
1 baguette, warmed and sliced

ASSEMBLY Heat 3 tablespoons oil in a skillet over medium heat. Add clams and squid and toss until coated. (Add more oil if necessary.) Cook for another minute, until juices evaporate. Add just enough stock to cover the seafood and bring to a boil. Cook for 1 to 2 minutes, until most of the clam shells have opened up. Whisk in butter and half the lemon juice and season with salt. Discard any unopened clams. Set aside.

Heat the remaining ¼ cup oil in another skillet over medium-high heat. Add scallops and sear for 3 minutes, until a golden crust forms on one side. Remove pan from heat, flip the scallops over, and set aside. (Do not overcook!)

Transfer clams and squid with the sauce to a large bowl and arrange scallops on top. Finish with salsa verde and a little lemon juice. Serve immediately with baguette.

AMAVI CELLARS
—
PEPPER BRIDGE WINERY

+

JEAN-FRANÇOIS PELLET

Powerful little wineries like Leonetti and L'Ecole N° 41 (page 146) made an instant impression on Jean-François Pellet (JF), who saw potential in Washington winemaking. Pepper Bridge Winery produced a single Merlot and Cabernet Sauvignon when it was launched in 1998 by Norm McKibben, Ray Goff, and JF. In 2008, they added to their portfolio a Bordeaux-style blend called Trine (a nod to the three partners), which was named a Top 100 Wine by *Wine & Spirits* in 2018 for the 2015 vintage. "Washington wines have the generosity of the New World with some of the intricacies of the Old World," JF explains. "And that's my style of wine."

In the early 2000s, JF, named Winemaker of the Year by the Washington Wine Awards in 2015, and his Pepper Bridge Winery partners opened another winery called Amavi Cellars, with the goal of producing great wines at a great price tag from their Estate Vineyards. "Each winery has different blocks from the vineyard and different [approaches to] winemaking and management." But the defining European-style characteristics are the same: the wines are always elegant and balanced. As a result, Amavi Cellars

has earned numerous accolades for the winery and its wines. In 2008 and 2014, Amavi Cellars wines were in the *Wine Spectator's* Top 100. And in 2007 and 2010, the winery was named a Top 100 Winery by *Wine & Spirits*, as was Pepper Bridge Winery in 2009–2012 and 2015–2016.

"You can enjoy our wines on their own, but they're definitely crafted in a way that allows them to be paired with food."

> *Smoked Lamb with White Cheddar Grits Soufflé* | *p. 30*

SMOKED LAMB
with White Cheddar Grits Soufflé

CHEF: BOBBY MOORE, BARKING FROG

Pictured p. 29

SERVES 4

WINE PAIRING: Amavi Cellars Syrah

Chef Bobby Moore created this serendipitous dish when he put some lamb on the smoker and forgot about it for six hours. "It turned out to be the best overcooked lamb," muses the chef. "I served it at the James Beard House the following year and received a standing ovation!" The key here is to frequently spray the lamb with a whiskey–apple juice marinade.

Lamb and Syrah make a classic pairing, and the spice and depth of the Amavi Cellars' Syrah cuts through the richness of the cheddar grits soufflé.

RED WINE ONIONS Combine vinegar and wine in a saucepan and bring to a simmer. Put onion in a bowl and pour in the hot liquid. Set aside for 1 hour. Refrigerate until needed.

SPICE RUB In a small bowl, combine all ingredients and mix well.

SMOKED RACK OF LAMB Rub lamb with Dijon mustard, then cover the entire surface with the spice rub. Refrigerate, uncovered, overnight. Remove lamb rack from the refrigerator 1 hour prior to cooking and bring to room temperature.

Preheat a smoker to 200°F. Place a handful of applewood chips and hickory on hot coals. Fill a drip pan with 2 inches of apple juice (about 3 cups), then set lamb chops on the grate and place in the smoker.

Smoke lamb for 5 hours, adding one to two handfuls of wood chips every hour. Remove lamb from the smoker, wrap in aluminum foil, then smoke for another hour. (Remove drip pan from smoker.) Pour the remaining 1 cup of apple juice and whiskey into a spray bottle. Every 20 to 30 minutes during the last hour of cooking, unwrap the lamb and spray it to help maintain moisture.

RED WINE ONIONS
½ cup red wine vinegar
½ cup red wine
1 red onion, thinly sliced

SPICE RUB
¼ cup dry mustard (preferably Coleman's)
3 Tbsp brown sugar
3 Tbsp black pepper
3 Tbsp kosher salt
2 Tbsp granulated garlic
2 Tbsp granulated sugar
1½ Tbsp smoked paprika
1 Tbsp ground cumin
1 Tbsp ground coriander
1 Tbsp dried rosemary

SMOKED RACK OF LAMB
3 lb rack of lamb, sliced into 8 chops
1½ cups Dijon mustard
1 quantity Spice Rub (see here)
5 handfuls applewood chips, pre-soaked in 2 cups apple juice (divided)
5 handfuls hickory chips, pre-soaked in 2 cups apple juice (divided)
4 cups apple juice (divided)
½ cup whiskey (preferably Jack Daniel's)

WHITE CHEDDAR GRITS SOUFFLÉ

6 Tbsp (¾ stick) cold butter, cut
  into ½-inch cubes, plus extra
  for greasing
4 cups whole milk
1 cup quick-cooking (not instant)
  grits
3 cups shredded white cheddar
  (8 oz)
½ cup thinly sliced chives
2 tsp kosher salt
Black pepper, to taste
6 eggs

WHITE CHEDDAR GRITS SOUFFLÉ Preheat oven to 350°F
and place rack in the middle. Grease four individual ramekins and set aside.

Heat milk in a large saucepan over medium-high heat and
bring to a boil. Add grits and whisk continuously. Reduce
heat to low and whisk for another 10 minutes, until thickened. Remove from heat.

Stir in cheddar, chives, butter, and salt until well mixed.
Season with pepper. Add eggs and stir until well mixed. Pour
into the prepared ramekins and bake for 15 to 20 minutes,
until puffed and golden.

ASSEMBLY Arrange lamb chops on each plate, spoon
red wine onions over the top, and serve immediately
with soufflé.

WHITE CHEDDAR AND GRUYÈRE MAC AND CHEESE
CHEF: BOBBY MOORE, BARKING FROG

MAC AND CHEESE
3 Tbsp kosher salt (divided)
1 lb gemelli pasta or your favorite
¼ cup (½ stick) butter
½ cup all-purpose flour
4 cups whole milk
3 cups heavy cream
2 lbs white cheddar (preferably
    Tillamook), shredded (8 cups)

ASSEMBLY
2 cups grated Gruyère (divided)
½ lb crispy cooked bacon,
    crumbled (optional)
1½ cups panko breadcrumbs
½ lb smoked salmon (optional)
Chopped parsley, for garnish
Chopped thyme, for garnish

WINE PAIRING: Pepper Bridge Trine

This Barking Frog staple is comfort food at its best. It has all the wonderfully satisfying elements of a traditional mac and cheese, but smoked salmon and bacon take it to another level. Here, chef Bobby Moore prepares it with gemelli—a single-stranded pasta that is folded in half and twisted—but any favorite pasta can be substituted.

Pepper Bridge Trine is a delicious Bordeaux-style blend of Cabernet Franc, Cabernet Sauvignon, Merlot, Petit Verdot, and Malbec. Notes of ripe red raspberry and cassis cut through the richness and accentuate the smokiness of the salmon. The velvety finish is as smooth as the texture of this dish itself.

MAC AND CHEESE Bring a large saucepan of water and 2 tablespoons salt to a boil. Add pasta and cook for 10 minutes, until pasta is al dente. Drain, then set aside.

Melt butter in a large saucepan over medium heat. Add flour and cook for 3 to 4 minutes, until golden and nutty. Whisk in milk and cream and bring to a boil. Cook for 3 minutes, stirring often, until golden brown. Stir in cheddar and the remaining 1 tablespoon salt for 2 minutes, until smooth. Combine pasta and cheese sauce.

ASSEMBLY Preheat oven to 350°F.

Transfer half of the mac and cheese into a Dutch oven or baking dish. Sprinkle 1 cup Gruyère and bacon, if using, on top. Add remaining mac and cheese, top with remaining Gruyère, and finish with breadcrumbs.

Bake for 10 minutes, until breadcrumbs are lightly browned and cheese is bubbly. Top with smoked salmon, if using, parsley, and thyme. Cool slightly, then serve.

ANDREW
JANUIK
WINES

+

ANDREW
JANUIK

Andrew Januik was destined to become a winemaker. His father, Mike Januik, a prestigious winemaker in his own right, was the winemaker at Chateau Ste. Michelle (page 64) when Andrew was young. Andrew's uncle, John Bigelow, is the owner and winemaker at neighboring JM Cellars. While other kids were playing Nintendo, Andrew was running around wineries.

In 1999, Mike started Januik Winery. "I was working in wineries from that point on," says Andrew, who started experimenting with winemaking when he was still in high school. In 2011, after a few years at Novelty Hill and Januik (two independent wineries under the same roof and led by Mike), Andrew started making his own wine.

"As the years have gone on, my wines have shifted in style: they're still supple medium-bodied wines, but more nuanced."

Andrew, who continues to make Januik wines along with his dad, was named one of both *Zagat*'s and *425 Magazine*'s "30 under 30" tastemakers in 2016. His first vintage—a 2011 Stone Cairn made from Red Mountain Cabernet Sauvignon—best exemplifies his winemaking. "I truly love Red Mountain grapes, and this wine demonstrates how fairly bold wines from that region can still be nuanced and elegant. Many Red Mountain wines, Stone Cairn

included, can be enjoyed alone or with a meal, making them incredibly versatile for wine consumers." He adds, "I learned to pick out a corked wine when I was nine years old. Wine will always be a part of our family culture. And I wouldn't have it any other way."

CAVATELLI with Braised Rabbit
and Chanterelles CHEF: AARON GRUND, NOVELTY HILL JANUIK

WINE PAIRING: Andrew Januik Los Molinos

Cavatelli are small pasta shells shaped like miniature hot dogs. Here, they are elevated with a decadent sauce made with rabbit, chanterelles, and Parmesan rinds. We love to pair it with Andrew Januik's Los Molinos, a bold wine with notes of cassis and cocoa and a bright finish that will stand up to the richness of this luscious dish.

PORCINI-BRAISED RABBIT Season the rabbit with salt and pepper and refrigerate overnight.

Preheat oven to 275°F.

Heat oil in a large saucepan over medium-high heat. Add rabbits and brown for 2 minutes on each side, until golden. (Cook in batches, if necessary, to avoid overcrowding.) Transfer rabbits to a roasting pan and set aside.

In the same saucepan, add onion and porcini (or other dried mushroom; no need to soak) and sauté for a minute. Season with salt and pepper, then pour in wine and cook for 2 to 3 minutes, until reduced by half. Add stock and bring to a boil.

Pour mixture into the roasting pan and add Parmesan rinds. Cook in the oven, covered, for 2½ hours, until meat easily pulls away from the bone. Remove from the oven and set aside to cool.

Transfer rabbits to a cutting board, then pick the meat off the bones and set aside. Discard bones. Strain braising liquid into a bowl and reserve for the sauce.

PORCINI-BRAISED RABBIT
3 (2-lb) whole rabbits
1 tsp kosher salt, plus extra to taste
1 tsp black pepper, plus extra to taste
5 Tbsp canola oil
2 yellow onions, chopped
4 cups dried porcini mushrooms or any other dried mushroom
1 cup dry white wine
5 cups chicken stock
2 cups Parmesan rinds (ask your local cheesemonger)

CAVATELLI PASTA

2½ cups all-purpose flour,
  plus extra for dusting
2½ cups semolina flour
1½ Tbsp kosher salt

SAGE RICOTTA

1 cup ricotta
1 Tbsp chopped sage leaves
1 tsp grated lemon zest
Salt and black pepper, to taste

ASSEMBLY

1 quantity Cavatelli Pasta
  (see here)
¼ cup (½ stick) butter (divided)
3 Tbsp sliced leeks
2 sage leaves, thinly sliced
1 large clove garlic, chopped
1 cup sliced chanterelle
  mushrooms
½ cup cooked chickpeas
Salt and black pepper, to taste
1½ cups rabbit-braising liquid
  (see here)
¼ cup Vin Santo or any
  dessert wine
2 Tbsp Sage Ricotta (see here)

CAVATELLI PASTA In a large bowl, combine flours and salt. Stir in 1 cup lukewarm water and knead for 5 minutes, until just combined (do not overknead). Form dough into a ball, wrap in plastic wrap, and set aside at room temperature for 1 hour.

Divide dough into four pieces. (Cover unused dough with a damp dish towel or plastic wrap to prevent the dough from drying out.) On a lightly floured counter, roll out a piece into a ½-inch-wide rope. Using a butter knife, cut it into ½-inch pieces.

Place each piece on a cavatelli paddle or gently press and roll down a dinner fork to create ridges on one side. Dust with flour to prevent sticking. (Makes about 4 cups.)

SAGE RICOTTA In a small bowl, combine all ingredients and set aside.

ASSEMBLY Bring a large saucepan of salted water to a boil. Add cavatelli and cook for 3 to 5 minutes, until nearly al dente.

Meanwhile, heat 2 tablespoons butter in a large skillet over medium-high heat and cook for 5 minutes, until brown. Add leeks, sage, garlic, and chanterelles and sauté for 1 minute, until mushrooms are lightly browned.

Add chickpeas and season with salt and pepper. Stir in rabbit meat and braising liquid and bring to a simmer.

Drain pasta, then add it to the skillet. Toss to coat, season with salt and pepper to taste, and cook for 3 to 4 minutes, until sauce has reduced slightly and coats the back of a spoon. Stir in Vin Santo (or any dessert wine).

Remove from heat and stir in the remaining 2 tablespoons of butter. Transfer pasta to warm serving bowls and garnish with a dollop of sage ricotta.

ROASTED SHALLOT
SOUP with Gorgonzola Croutons

CHEF: AARON GRUND, NOVELTY HILL JANUIK

3 sprigs marjoram, plus extra
    for garnish
2 sprigs thyme, plus extra for
    garnish
1 bay leaf
¼ cup (½ stick) butter
5 large shallots, thinly sliced
1 Tbsp kosher salt
½ cup red wine
½ cup Madeira
6 cups veal stock
1 Tbsp sherry vinegar
Salt and black pepper, to taste
¼ cup cognac
6 slices baguette
1 cup crumbled Gorgonzola or
    blue cheese (such as Rogue
    Creamery's Rogue River Blue)

WINE PAIRING: Andrew Januik Lady Hawk

A play on traditional French onion soup, this cold-weather essential combines sweet and savory for a rich, full-bodied broth. The Cabernet Sauvignon–heavy Lady Hawk has well-balanced tannins and spice notes to pair nicely with this fortifying meal in a bowl.

Tie marjoram, thyme, and bay leaf with kitchen twine.

Melt butter in a heavy-bottomed saucepan over medium-low heat. Add shallot, herbs, and salt and cook for 15 minutes, stirring occasionally, until shallot just begins to caramelize.

Increase heat to medium-high, then add wine and Madeira and cook for 3 to 4 minutes, until reduced by half. Pour in stock and cook for another 20 minutes. Add vinegar and season with salt and pepper to taste. Remove from heat and discard the herbs. Stir in cognac.

Preheat broiler to 400°F.

Arrange baguette slices on a baking sheet and broil for 1 minute on each side, until golden. Top each with Gorgonzola (or blue cheese) and broil for another minute, until cheese starts to melt. (Be careful not to burn the bread.)

Ladle soup into bowls and top with a baguette slice. Garnish with marjoram or thyme and serve immediately.

ANICHE CELLARS

✛

RACHAEL HORN AND ANAIS MERA

The Great American Novel is on hold for Rachael Horn, who traded writer's block for a vineyard block back in 2009.

Wine, the muse that fueled her creativity as an author for years, became the impetus behind her family-run winery in Underwood, a stunning location that overlooks the Columbia River Gorge. A mash-up of Anais and Che (the respective names of her daughter and son), AniChe is the result of Rachael's storied history with wine—an idea that initially sprang from her time as a server at the Columbia Gorge Hotel in Hood River, Oregon. One night, a customer, keen on Rachael's deep knowledge of wine, encouraged her to pursue winemaking. "I was waiting tables, saving for a trip to Europe, and supposedly writing my next book," Rachael reveals. "It was truly an epiphanous moment."

As one of the first female winemakers in the Gorge, Rachael and her daughter, Anais, started making wines to fill a gap. "Washington wines were big, jammy, alcoholic, and richer. I wanted to make European-style blends."

Drawing on Rachael's love of prose, each wine is named after a literary character. There's Atticus (Finch), Goat Boy (*Where the Wild Things Are*), Be Holden (Holden Caulfield), and more. And just like those characters, there's life—personality, color, texture—to Rachael's wines.

"What the vineyard gives us is what we make. We're witchy that way," she shares. "And what happens in the vineyard, we give back to you—we want you to be able to drink that year." In other words, each wine has its own narrative.

ROCKFISH TARTARE BRUSCHETTA with Nectarines, Whey, Chile, and Basil CHEF: ZOI ANTONITSAS

¼ cup whey or buttermilk
2 Tbsp lemon juice
½ tsp granulated sugar
½ tsp kosher salt
1 lb sashimi-grade skinless
    rockfish, snapper, or bass
    fillets, cut into ¼-inch dice
2 medium-large nectarines (about
    1 lb), unpeeled and cut into
    ¼-inch dice
1 shallot, finely chopped
1 Fresno chile, stem removed,
    deseeded, and finely chopped
4 (½-inch-thick) slices good-
    quality bread, such as French
    sourdough or walnut bread
¼ cup good-quality extra-virgin
    olive oil (divided)
⅓ cup small basil leaves, torn,
    plus extra for garnish
½ tsp finishing salt

WINE PAIRING: AniChe Come & Go Albariño

Bursting with tropical fruit, gooseberry, and nectarine, AniChe's Come & Go Albariño has a sweet and savory profile with smooth, rounded flavor and salty minerality—not unlike this bruschetta. Chef Zoi Antonitsas enjoys serving this on a warm summer evening, preferably outdoors, by the sea.

In a glass or stainless-steel bowl, combine whey, lemon juice, sugar, and salt. Add fish and toss to coat. Cover and refrigerate for up to 4 hours.

Preheat grill to high heat.

In a large bowl, combine nectarines, shallot, and chile. Gently fold in the fish, then refrigerate for 15 minutes.

Meanwhile, grill the bread for 1 minute on each side, until nicely browned. Drizzle 2 tablespoons oil on top. Remove bowl from refrigerator and add basil. Add the remaining 2 tablespoons oil and gently fold.

Spoon tartare over the bread, garnish with basil, and drizzle the excess liquid (also known as "tiger's milk") on top. Sprinkle with finishing salt and serve immediately.

SALT AND PEPPER CHOCOLATE COOKIES

with Dried Cherry CHEF: ZOI ANTONITSAS

WINE PAIRING: AniChe Moth Love

These decadent cookies are a fun conclusion to a cocktail party, casual dinner, or even a weeknight treat. Chef Zoi Antonitsas, who loves savory notes with desserts, combines salt and chocolate and adds cherries and walnuts for texture. The pepper lends a little heat and an element of surprise.

The soft notes of bushberries, tobacco, oak, and warm spices create the backbone of this delicious juicy red blend. Simply bake the cookies, open a bottle of wine, and call it a night! The cookies can be stored in an airtight container for up to a week.

½ cup (1 stick) butter, room temperature
½ cup + 2 Tbsp granulated sugar
1 egg, room temperature
½ tsp vanilla extract
1 cup + 2 Tbsp all-purpose flour
¼ cup cocoa powder
2 tsp flaky sea salt
1 tsp black pepper
½ tsp baking powder
4 oz good-quality dark or semisweet chocolate, chopped
¼ cup dried Washington cherries, chopped
¼ cup chopped walnuts (optional)

Preheat oven to 350°F. Line a baking sheet with parchment paper.

In a large bowl, cream butter and sugar. Beat in egg and vanilla.

In a separate bowl, combine flour, cocoa powder, salt, pepper, and baking powder. Add dry ingredients to wet ingredients and mix well. Stir in chocolate, cherries, and walnuts, if using. Using your hands, knead dough together (the dough will be very thick).

Using a spoon or small ice cream scoop, place golf-ball-sized mounds of dough (about 2 tablespoons) onto the prepared baking sheet, evenly spacing them 2 inches apart. Roll each into a ball, then gently flatten into a ½-inch-thick patty. Bake for 9 to 12 minutes, until cookies are golden.

BROOK & BULL CELLARS

+

ASHLEY TROUT

Ashley Trout has always had a sense of wanderlust. At the age of eighteen, she moved from Washington, DC, to attend Whitman College in Walla Walla—not because she had a drive to be in the wine industry, but because she wanted to experience the charm of a small agricultural community.

During her first year of school, she worked part-time at a winery. The following year, she took a semester off to work the harvest full-time "because I was fascinated by the snapshot of this changing entity and I wanted to see the whole story." By her third and fourth harvests, she was hooked.

But it took sustaining a near fatal rock-climbing accident before what would have been her fifth harvest to solidify her decision to make wine for a living. "It felt wrong to [simply] watch harvest happen around me, and that fifth harvest taught me how depressing and unfulfilling any other path would be."

In 2005, toward the end of her eight-year run at Reininger Winery, she launched her own label, Flying Trout. She sold it after a couple years and stayed on as winemaker for five more years before starting Brook & Bull (both are types of trout) and Vital Wines in 2016. Vital is a nonprofit winery helping to improve access to healthcare for vineyard and winery workers.

"My palate skews towards a little more acid, which adds to the structure of a wine. It contributes to the aging process, makes a wine more food friendly, and elevates the entire experience." Ashley also doesn't shy away from the pyrazines that give wines vegetable or green-pepper notes. "As a boutique winery, we can make the wines we want, and our tribe can find us if we do our job right."

FRIED SUNCHOKES
with Blue-Cheese Dressing

CHEF: BRENDAN MCGILL, HITCHCOCK

2 quarts olive oil, for deep-frying
2 lbs organic sunchokes, scrubbed
1 cup aioli or high-quality
   mayonnaise
1 cup crème fraîche or organic
   Greek yogurt
½ cup crumbled blue cheese,
   such as Rogue Creamery's
   Smokey Blue
Handful of soft herbs, such
   as chives, oregano, chervil,
   parsley, dill, tarragon, lovage,
   or mint
Finishing salt, to taste

WINE PAIRING: Brook & Bull Malbec

Sunchokes, also known as Jerusalem artichokes, are the unsung heroes of the tuber family. According to etymological lore, Italians brought them from the Old World and referred to them as *girasole* (sunflower), since the plant bore resemblance to the sunflower (minus the giant blossom). Apparently, the term was misheard as "Jerusalem," and because they taste a bit like artichokes, they became Jerusalem artichokes.

This notably restrained Malbec pairs beautifully with mushrooms and blue cheese. The earthy nature of the sunchokes draws out the tobacco and spices in the wine, while the blue cheese brightens the subdued plums.

Heat oil in a deep fryer or deep saucepan over medium heat to 275°F. Carefully lower sunchokes into the hot oil, working in batches to avoid overcrowding (and reducing the temperature of the oil). Deep-fry for 4 to 6 minutes, until tender. (To check doneness, remove a sunchoke from the oil. If it can be easily pierced with a skewer, it's ready.) Using a slotted spoon, transfer sunchokes onto a wire rack, spaced out, and set aside.

In a bowl, combine aioli (or mayonnaise), crème fraîche (or yogurt), blue cheese, and herbs, leaving some herbs for the garnish. Refrigerate until cooled.

Increase the temperature of the deep-frying oil to 375°F. Using the palm of your hand, gently press on each sunchoke to break the skin and flatten it slightly. (This creates more surface area to crisp up.) Carefully lower sunchokes into the oil and deep-fry for 4 to 6 minutes, until crispy and golden brown. Using a slotted spoon, transfer to a wire rack lined with paper towels. (Leftover oil can be strained through a coffee filter or fine-mesh strainer and funneled back into the bottle. Label it "fry oil" and reuse it when needed.) Season with salt.

Transfer sunchokes to a serving dish and garnish with herbs. Serve with the blue-cheese dressing.

GAMBAS
A LA PLANCHA

CHEF: BRENDAN MCGILL, HITCHCOCK

24 live spot prawns
Good-quality olive oil, for
    drizzling
Sea salt, to taste
Pinch of sweet smoked paprika
    (pimentón de la Vera dulce)
    (optional)

WINE PAIRING: Brook & Bull Rosé

This popular tapas dish is ubiquitous in Spain, served everywhere from tiny beer stands to fine restaurants. A *plancha* is a hot plank of steel that is set over an open flame, but you can also use a cast-iron skillet. Brook & Bull's dry, quaffable rosé makes a suitable companion with just enough fruit to enhance the flavors in the prawns. Chef Brendan McGill highly recommends purchasing spot prawns when they're in season from a fish company with a live tank, such as Uwajimaya, Central Market, or Mutual Fish.

With one hand, hold a spot prawn upright but flat on a surface. With a knife in the other hand, pierce through the top of the head into the brain and split the head in half. (Hold the prawn tight; it'll be jumpy.) Repeat with remaining prawns.

Rinse prawns well under cold running water, then lay them flat on a dry towel.

Heat a plancha or cast-iron skillet over high heat until hot. Have oil and salt on standby. Add prawns to the pan, then generously sprinkle with salt. Drizzle a thin line of oil across prawns (it will create a dramatic sizzle) and cook for a few seconds, until a brown crust from the prawn juice solidifies on the shell. (Be careful not to overcook.) Flip the prawns over and cook for another 30 seconds, until tail meat is just cooked and translucent in the center. Add paprika, if using.

Transfer prawns to a serving platter, sprinkle with more paprika if desired, and serve immediately. To eat the spot prawns, crack the head from the body and peel shell from the tail meat. Of course the tail meat is delicious, but the real treat is in the head's "guts," which taste like a shrimpier version of lobster tomalley.

BROWNE FAMILY VINEYARDS

+

JOHN FREEMAN

John Freeman—who grew up in Napa, California—laid the groundwork for winemaking when he was in the third grade. John's older brother had discovered fermentation from his fifth-grade teacher.

"He came home with his new-found knowledge, and we'd ferment stuff such as apple juice from the refrigerator or apple cider. We would crush blackberries in the backyard and sprinkle baking yeast on them because that's all we had. And that went on for years."

As John got older and realized he enjoyed wine, he took a job on the bottling line at a winery. "The manager gave me a bottle of wine at the end of my first day. It was actually the first bottle of wine I ever had that had a cork!"

In the early 2000s, as Napa continued to expand and become more crowded, John moved to Walla Walla, where he took a job as assistant winemaker at Waterbrook Winery. In 2005, he became head winemaker. The following year, he tacked on another title as head winemaker for Browne Family Vineyards, founder Andrew Browne's tribute to his grandfather, William Bitner Browne. Both are owned by Andrew and his company, Precept Wine.

"When we first started making wines for Browne Family Vineyards, we were producing the best Cabernet we could make. As time went on, we added a red blend, a Merlot, a Chardonnay, and noble Bordeaux styles, and we've been expanding ever since."

Free wine still keeps John going, but more than that, he likes the ever-changing aspect of the industry. Nothing is ever scripted. "There's always something new to discover: something new to taste, a new vineyard to look at, and new ideas of vines to plant."

> *Beef Keftas with Eggplant Purée, Mint, and Pickled Onion* | *p. 50*

BEEF KEFTAS with Eggplant
Purée, Mint, and Pickled Onion

CHEF: ERIC DONNELLY, FLINTCREEK

Pictured p. 49

SERVES 6 TO 8

WINE PAIRING: Browne Family Vineyards Cabernet Sauvignon

Browne Family's Cabernet Sauvignon—a powerful and complex expression of Washington Cabernet Sauvignon—is capable of standing up to the boldest dishes. The bold tannins and dark fruit perfectly balance the intricate spices of the beef keftas, while still complementing the umami richness of the eggplant and the sweetness of the pickled onions. At FlintCreek, chef Eric Donnelly uses tenderloin, hanger, and rib-eye trim for the keftas, but a high-quality grind from a good butcher will also do nicely.

PICKLED RED ONION In a small nonreactive saucepan, combine wine, sugar, cloves, bay leaf, and salt and bring to a slow simmer over medium heat. Add onion, bring to simmer again, and cook for 30 seconds. Set aside to cool.

EGGPLANT PURÉE Preheat oven to 400°F. Line a baking sheet with parchment paper.

Place eggplants on a cutting board or plate, generously drizzle oil all over, and season with salt. Arrange eggplants, face down, on the prepared baking sheet and bake for 10 minutes, until very soft and cooked through. Set aside to cool.

Using a large spoon, scrape out the flesh and put into a small food processor. (Makes about 2 cups.) Add tahini, lemon juice, sesame oil, and paprika. Purée until smooth and season with salt to taste.

PICKLED RED ONION
1 cup red wine
½ cup granulated sugar
2 whole cloves
1 bay leaf
Pinch of salt
1 small red onion, thinly sliced

EGGPLANT PURÉE
2 Japanese eggplants, halved
   lengthwise
Olive oil, for drizzling
Salt
¼ cup tahini paste
1 Tbsp lemon juice
1 tsp sesame oil
1 tsp smoked paprika

1 lb high-quality ground beef
1 onion, finely chopped
3 cloves garlic, finely chopped
2 Tbsp grated ginger
½ cup crushed pine nuts
¼ cup finely chopped parsley
¼ cup finely chopped mint
2 tsp ground cinnamon
1 tsp Aleppo pepper
1 tsp ground cumin
1 tsp ground coriander
½ tsp ground cloves
1 tsp kosher salt
1 egg yolk
2 Tbsp olive oil

ASSEMBLY

Mint leaves, torn, for garnish
Aleppo pepper, for sprinkling
Finishing salt, for sprinkling

BEEF KEFTAS In a large stainless-steel bowl, combine beef, onion, garlic, ginger, pine nuts, parsley, and mint. Add spices and salt and mix well. Add egg yolk and stir.

Portion mixture into ¼-cup balls, then gently roll them into oblong shapes. Add these keftas, lengthwise, to bamboo skewers or metal kebabs.

Heat oil in a large cast-iron skillet over medium-high heat. Add skewers and cook for 2 to 3 minutes. Turn over and cook for another 2 to 4 minutes, until meat is cooked to medium.

ASSEMBLY On a serving plate or shallow bowl, spread out the eggplant purée. Arrange skewers on top, then garnish with pickled onions, mint, Aleppo pepper, and salt.

PAN-FRIED DUNGENESS CRAB

with Tomalley Aioli CHEF: ERIC DONNELLY, FLINTCREEK

SERVES 2 TO 4

WINE PAIRING: Browne Family Vineyards Chardonnay

While this fantastic dish speaks to the flavors of summer, live Dungeness crabs are available year-round at reputable seafood markets or high-end grocery stores. Chef Eric Donnelly dredges the crab in Wondra flour—a flour blend made up of wheat and malted barley—to yield extra crispy results.

And a rich dish like this needs to be paired with a full-bodied white. Browne Family's Chardonnay steps to the plate with its bright citrus notes and tartness.

DUNGENESS CRAB In a stockpot, add all ingredients except for the crab. Pour in 1 gallon (4 quarts) water and bring to a boil over high heat. Cook for 5 minutes.

Add the crab and cook for 14 to 21 minutes (7 minutes per pound). Transfer the crab to a baking sheet with the legs up and shell down. (This prevents the meat from turning grey and unattractive.) Place in the refrigerator and chill until needed.

TOMALLEY AIOLI Over a large bowl, remove the crab shell, separating the legs from the head, and reserve the top shell for garnish. Strain all innards through a fine-mesh strainer and reserve (this is the tomalley). (Yields about 1 cup.) Discard the lungs and small shell pieces.

In a small saucepan, combine tomalley, saffron, vinegar, and lemon juice and cook over medium-low heat for 4 to 5 minutes, until vibrant and reduced by two-thirds. Transfer mixture to a bowl and refrigerate until chilled.

In a blender or food processor, combine tomalley-saffron paste, egg yolk, and salt. With the motor running on medium speed, gradually pour in oil until emulsified.

DUNGENESS CRAB
1 lemon, halved
1 orange, halved
1 jalapeño, halved lengthwise
½ white onion
4 cloves garlic
¼ cup kosher or sea salt
2 Tbsp pickling spice
1 Tbsp Old Bay Seasoning
1 cup white wine vinegar
1 (2- to 3-lb) live Dungeness crab

TOMALLEY AIOLI
Reserved Dungeness Crab, chilled (see here)
8 saffron threads
1 Tbsp white wine vinegar
Juice of 1 lemon
1 egg yolk
1 tsp kosher salt
1½ cups grapeseed or any neutral-flavored oil

1 cup Wondra flour
1 Tbsp kosher salt
1 tsp ground white pepper
1 tsp cayenne pepper
3 Tbsp extra-virgin olive oil
2 cloves garlic, sliced
10 basil leaves
8 lemon slices, full rounds
   with no seeds

ASSEMBLY In a large bowl, combine flour, salt, white pepper, and cayenne. Quarter crab into two-leg sections, then add them to the bowl and dredge.

Heat oil in a large skillet over medium-high heat. Add crab and cook each side for 2 minutes, until legs are caramelized. Add garlic and toast for 1 minute, until light brown. Add basil and fry for 30 seconds, until crispy. Add lemon slices.

Spread tomalley aioli on a serving platter. Using tongs, arrange crab legs on top and garnish with fried basil, garlic chips, and lemon slices. Serve immediately.

CAIRDEAS WINERY

+

CHARLIE AND LACEY LYBECKER

"I didn't know anything about wine until I met Lacey," says Charlie Lybecker, who was working as a website developer and audio engineer for the radio industry when he and Lacey started dating in 2005. They both dreamed of one day trading in their desk jobs to pursue something more ambitious.

Lacey, whose fascination with wine was sparked by a trip to Australia's Yarra Valley, introduced Charlie to different varieties. "We would sample a varietal of wine that was made by different producers in the same part of the world, and they all tasted different," Charlie recalls. "And because I'm curious and like to know how things work, I was intrigued. That's what got me into wine."

As their relationship—with each other and with wine—intensified, they started experimenting with winemaking in their garage in West Seattle. That's when Lacey says Charlie got bit by the wine bug. When he suggested that they start a winery when they retire, she replied, "Let's start one right now!" The two got their West Seattle garage bonded and did just that.

Cairdeas (pronounced *KAHR-diss*) is Gaelic for "friendship" or "goodwill." It's a way for Charlie and Lacey, both of Irish descent, to pay homage to their families. The couple moved to Lake Chelan in 2012.

"I fell in love with Syrah and Viognier, which are both Rhône varietals, when we were studying Washington wines," says Charlie, who's since added lesser-known Rhône varieties like Cinsault and Counoise to their lineup. "The wines are elegant with hints of spice."

If you had asked Charlie two decades ago if he thought he'd be a winemaker, he'd tell you it was just a pipe dream. "I didn't believe it would happen, and I am very thankful it's become our reality."

OCTOPUS with Smoky Bacon, Fish-Sauce Caramel, and Ramp Salsa Verde CHEF: AARON TEKULVE, SURRELL

FISH-SAUCE CARAMEL
½ cup granulated sugar
2 Tbsp corn syrup
1 clove garlic, finely chopped
3 Tbsp fish sauce
1 tsp grated ginger
1 tsp finely chopped shallot
1 tsp serrano chile, finely
  chopped

WILD RAMP SALSA VERDE
1 Tbsp grapeseed or canola oil
1 cup chopped ramps or scallions
1 clove garlic, finely chopped
¼ cup chopped cilantro
1 tsp finely chopped shallot
¼ cup fruity extra-virgin olive oil
  (preferably Arbequina)
Grated zest and juice of 1 lime
Salt and black pepper, to taste

OCTOPUS WITH SMOKY BACON
4 bay leaves
1 large yellow onion, quartered
1 head garlic, halved
2 Tbsp kosher salt, plus extra to
  taste
2 (1- to 2-lb) fresh whole
  octopuses
½ lb smoked bacon (preferably
  Nueske's Applewood Smoked),
  cut into thin strips

ASSEMBLY
¾ cup Fish-Sauce Caramel (see
  here)
1 cup Wild Ramp Salsa Verde
  (see here)
Cilantro leaves, for garnish

WINE PAIRING: Cairdeas Winery Caislén an Pápa

The combination of octopus, bacon, and fish sauce, along with the ramps, is a signature of Aaron's cooking. The unusual fish-sauce caramel might raise brows, but trust us, it works perfectly well with octopus and bacon. The Caislén an Pápa has great pairing diversity: the acidity and depth of flavor cut through the richness of the dish.

FISH-SAUCE CARAMEL In a small saucepan, combine sugar, corn syrup, and ¼ cup water and bring to a boil over high heat. Cook for 5 to 7 minutes, swirling the pot, until dark amber and the temperature reaches 340°F on a candy thermometer.

Add the remaining ingredients and another ¼ cup water. Once the mixture stops bubbling, stir, remove from heat, and keep at room temperature until use. (Makes ¾ cup.)

WILD RAMP SALSA VERDE Heat oil in a skillet set over medium-low heat. Add ramps (or scallions) and sauté for 2 to 3 minutes, until just wilted. Set aside to cool.

In a small bowl, combine the remaining ingredients, add ramps, and mix well. Season with salt and pepper.

OCTOPUS WITH SMOKY BACON Heat a stockpot of water over high heat. Add bay leaves, onion, garlic, and salt and bring to a boil. Add octopus and boil vigorously, uncovered, for 75 to 90 minutes, until tender with a little chew. (Cut off a tentacle and slice a piece. If the texture is rubbery, cook octopus for another 15 minutes.) Transfer octopus to a bowl and set aside to cool, then remove tentacles.

Heat a skillet over medium heat. Add bacon and cook for 7 to 10 minutes, until crisp and well rendered. Add the tentacles and sauté for 3 to 5 minutes, until tentacles are warmed through and well coated in fat.

ASSEMBLY Reheat the caramel over low heat. Place a spoonful of salsa verde on a plate, then arrange two tentacles over it. Drizzle fish-sauce caramel on top and garnish with cilantro.

SPRING SALAD with Roasted
Shallot Vinaigrette, Chèvre, and Mint

CHEF: AARON TEKULVE, SURRELL

**ROASTED SHALLOT
VINAIGRETTE**

2 Tbsp grapeseed or rice bran oil
8 large shallots, chopped (2 cups)
4 large cloves garlic, chopped
1 cup fruity extra-virgin olive oil
   (preferably Arbequina)
⅓ cup sherry vinegar

SPRING SALAD

1 lb asparagus, trimmed and
   snapped, cut into 1-inch pieces
   (2 cups)
2 cups snap peas, trimmed and
   halved widthwise
Large bunch of broccolini, cut
   into ½-inch pieces (2 cups)
6 radishes, cut into eighths
   (½ cup)
1 large shallot, finely chopped
   (¼ cup)
½ cup finely chopped mint
1 cup Roasted Shallot Vinaigrette
   (see here), plus extra if needed
Salt and black pepper, to taste
2 cups crumbled chèvre (goat
   cheese)

WINE PAIRING: Cairdeas Winery Grenache Blanc

Spring is chef Aaron Tekulve's favorite season in the Pacific
Northwest. It's a time when fresh green vegetables come to
life, and come April or May, you'll find flavorful veg such as
the miniature Yakima Valley asparagus, sweet snap peas, and
spicy red radishes at the farmers' market. This salad is a celebration of those seasonal flavors and complemented with a
pleasing wine hinted with citrus notes.

ROASTED SHALLOT VINAIGRETTE Heat oil in a saucepan
over medium heat. Add shallot and sauté for 10 minutes,
until golden brown and caramelized. Add garlic and sauté
for 1 minute.

Transfer mixture to a blender and set aside to cool.
With the motor running, gradually add oil and vinegar and
blend until smooth. Refrigerate until needed. (Makes about
1½ cups.)

Leftover dressing can be stored in an airtight container
in the refrigerator for up to 2 months.

SPRING SALAD In a large bowl, combine asparagus, snap
peas, broccolini, radishes, shallot, and mint. Pour in vinaigrette, season with salt and pepper, and toss. Season with
more salt and pepper to taste.

Transfer salad to a large serving bowl and garnish with
chèvre.

CASTILLO DE FELICIANA

+

CHRISTOPHER CASTILLO

In a sea of Bordeaux- and Rhône-style wines, Castillo de Feliciana boasts standout Spanish varieties such as Tempranillo, Albariño, and the lesser-known Graciano, an obscure Rioja varietal. "As a Spanish-style winery, we use yeast from Spain," says the winemaker Christopher Castillo, the son of Deborah and Sam Castillo who started the winery in 2007. "And there's one type from Rioja that really enhances the earthiness and spiciness of Tempranillo." It works for the winery—their 2014 Reserve Tempranillo was awarded a Double Gold at the 2017 Seattle Wine Awards.

The idea for the winery was born years ago when Sam, who owned a dental practice in Duvall, was making wine in the family's garage. His experimental batch turned into a barrel and then eventually a nearly seven-acre vineyard in Walla Walla. They named the winery after Deborah's great-aunt Feliciana, whose legacy is carried on through the winery.

In 2010, Chris was brewing beer at Mac & Jack's Brewing Company in Redmond, Washington. He decided to study enology and viticulture at Walla Walla Community College and spent more time at the winery to get a better sense of the process. "My goal was to gain a better understanding of winemaking," he shares. "Wine was always in the family, and as a lover of fermentation, I've always been intrigued by winemaking." He made up his mind. He decided to join the family winery.

Chris has now been a winemaker longer than a professional brewer, but he still loves to brew beer at home. "You know what they say— it takes a lot of beer to make great wine!"

> Lamb Shanks with Chorizo and Creamy Manchego Polenta | p. 60

LAMB SHANKS with Chorizo
and Creamy Manchego Polenta

CHEF: EMELIO SANSONE, PINTXO

Pictured p. 59

SERVES 6

WINE PAIRING: Castillo de Feliciana Tempranillo

This rustic dish is full of bold, feel-good flavors that marry beautifully with a fine Tempranillo, and Castillo de Feliciana's wine offers a robust burst of jammy berries and spiced notes with every sip. With hints of bittersweet cocoa and oak bouncing back and forth through the pairing, flavors are rounded out in a profound finish on the tongue.

LAMB SHANK Preheat oven to 300°F.

In a small bowl, combine ½ tablespoon salt, cumin, and pepper. Pat lamb shanks dry, then rub in cumin seasoning.

Heat oil in a skillet or heavy-bottomed saucepan over medium-high heat. Add lamb shanks and brown all over, making sure not to burn the meat. Remove from heat.

Pour wine and vinegar into a Dutch oven and boil for 5 minutes. Add lamb shanks, garlic, bay leaves, orange, cinnamon, rosemary, lavender, peppercorns, paprika, stock, and orange juice. Cover and bring to a boil. Put the Dutch oven into the oven and cook for 2 hours. (Avoid opening the oven door, as this will drastically affect cooking time.)

Remove Dutch oven from the oven. Add chorizo, carrots, and onion. Season to taste by adding more salt and/or vinegar. Cover, return to the oven, and cook for 1 hour, until meat is tender and falls off the bone.

LAMB SHANK

½ Tbsp kosher salt, plus extra to taste
1 tsp ground cumin
½ tsp black pepper
6 lamb shanks
¼ cup canola oil, for frying
2 cups Tempranillo or Rioja
1 cup sherry vinegar, plus extra to taste
12 cloves garlic, crushed
2 bay leaves
1 orange, halved
1 stick cinnamon
3 sprigs rosemary
Sprig of lavender
2 tsp black peppercorns
1 to 2 tsp smoked paprika
2 cups beef stock
1¼ cups orange juice
8 to 12 oz Spanish chorizo, diced
2 carrots, sliced into rounds
1 red onion, chopped

4 cups whole milk, plus extra if
   needed

2 cups chicken stock

2½ tsp kosher salt

1½ cups medium-ground polenta
   or cornmeal (see Note)

1 tsp smoked paprika

¾ cup finely grated Manchego
   cheese

¼ cup (½ stick) butter

ASSEMBLY

Crème fraîche

Finely chopped parsley, chives, or
   mint, for garnish

NOTE: Instant polenta
can be used in a pinch,
but it won't yield the
same rich results.

CREAMY MANCHEGO POLENTA Combine milk, stock, and
salt in a medium saucepan set over medium heat. Slowly
pour in polenta (or cornmeal) and whisk continuously. Stir
in paprika and simmer for 20 to 25 minutes, until thickened,
stirring frequently to prevent sticking and burning. Remove
from heat.

Stir in Manchego and butter. If polenta is too thick, thin it
out with a little milk. If it is too thin, cook over low heat for
a few minutes longer. Keep warm.

ASSEMBLY Using a slotted spoon, carefully transfer lamb
shanks to a warm plate and set aside.

Boil braising liquid over high heat for 8 minutes, until
slightly thickened. Remove from heat, then season with salt
to taste.

Scoop 1 cup of polenta onto each serving plate. Arrange
a lamb shank and stewed vegetables on top. Generously
ladle sauce on top, add a dollop of crème fraîche, and garnish with fresh herbs. Serve warm.

TUNA with Romesco Sauce and
Roasted Fingerlings CHEF: EMELIO SANSONE, PINTXO

SERVES 4

WINE PAIRING: Castillo de Feliciana Albariño

This is a quick and easy dish to put together when you're looking for a savory springtime midweek meal. Chef Emelio Sansone loves to pair it with Albariño—the wine's subtle yet poignant citrus tones complement the sweet and lightly smoky sauce, its minerality forming a beautiful bridge of flavor from the very first bite.

FINGERLING POTATOES Preheat oven to 400°F.

Heat oil in a large ovenproof skillet over medium heat. Add garlic and sauté for 30 seconds, until fragrant. Remove garlic from oil using a finely slotted spoon and set aside. Add potatoes and cook for 1 minute, until potatoes begin to brown. Sprinkle rosemary, cumin, salt, and pepper over potatoes and stir, making sure the potatoes are evenly coated in oil. Transfer skillet to the middle rack in the oven and roast for 12 to 15 minutes.

Remove potatoes from oven, stir in peppers and reserved garlic, and return to the oven. Cook for another 5 to 10 minutes, until potatoes are lightly golden and fork tender. Keep warm.

TUNA WITH ROMESCO SAUCE Put tuna in a bowl. Lightly and evenly sprinkle 1 tablespoon salt over the tuna and mix well. Set aside.

In a food processor or blender, combine the remaining ingredients except for the oil but including the remaining 1 tablespoon salt, and pulse to combine. With the motor running, gradually add all but 2 tablespoons of oil and blend until emulsified.

FINGERLING POTATOES
2 Tbsp olive oil
1 Tbsp chopped garlic
1 lb fingerling potatoes, halved lengthwise
2 tsp chopped rosemary
½ tsp ground cumin
1 tsp kosher salt
¼ tsp black pepper
½ cup canned piquillo peppers or roasted red peppers, chopped

TUNA WITH ROMESCO SAUCE
2 lbs fresh tuna or any other firm fish, cut into 1-inch cubes
2 Tbsp kosher salt (divided), plus extra to taste
3 roasted red peppers, chopped
¼ to ½ cup Marcona almonds
6 cloves garlic, chopped
2 Tbsp chopped parsley
1 Tbsp chopped mint
1 Tbsp sweet paprika
1 tsp smoked paprika
1 tsp chopped oregano
Black pepper, to taste
¾ cup white wine
2 Tbsp sherry vinegar
1 Tbsp lemon juice
½ cup olive oil (divided)

Chopped parsley, for garnish
Finishing salt, for sprinkling
Extra-virgin olive oil, for drizzling
½ lemon

Heat the remaining 2 tablespoons oil in a large skillet over medium-high heat, making sure the oil does not smoke. Pat the tuna chunks dry with paper towels, then add tuna to the pan, a few at a time. Sear one side for 1 to 2 minutes, until it releases from the pan with little to no resistance. Using tongs, turn and sear for another minute, until it develops a crisp sear. (If the oil is not hot enough or the fish is too wet when placed into the pan, the fish will be more likely to stick.) Repeat with the remaining tuna.

Pour in the sauce and toss to evenly coat. Bring to a light boil, then simmer on low for 5 to 10 minutes. Season with salt and pepper to taste.

ASSEMBLY Divide potatoes among four plates. Arrange tuna over potatoes. Garnish with parsley, sprinkle with salt, and add a drizzle of oil. Finish with a good squeeze of lemon and serve immediately.

CHATEAU STE. MICHELLE

+

BOB BERTHEAU

Bob Bertheau's introduction into the wine business began with an old law in Idaho. While he was studying pre-med at Boise State University, he was working part-time at a tasting room. He was nineteen years old, the state's legal drinking age back then in the 1980s. He had already taken the entrance exam to med school when he realized it was time to make some serious decisions. "While working at the tasting room, someone told me that I could do this wine thing for a living," says Bob. "So I did some research and decided to combine my chemistry degree with my newfound passion for and knowledge of wine." The rest is history.

Considered the patriarch of Washington wine, Chateau Ste. Michelle (CSM) is the state's oldest wine producer. It was founded as the American Wine Growers in 1954, with its first vintage released in 1967 as

Ste. Michelle Vineyards. In 1976, the winery built its Woodinville Chateau and changed its name to Chateau Ste. Michelle. Their wines are now sold in more than a hundred countries.

As the leading producer of Riesling, they produce a staggering million cases a year. And yet, it's not the only wine they're known for—CSM's wines are diverse in style and varietals. For Bob, the wines must be approachable enough to want another glass or a second bottle. They also need to impress at their price point. "Our wines are complex and layered and not just simple fruit and oak, which is available at our price points."

CSM has wrangled some of the highest accolades in the wine industry, including *Wine & Spirits* magazine's Top 100 Wineries of the Year award (twenty-two times and counting). Eighteen of their wines have appeared on *Wine Spectator*'s prestigious Top 100 Wines list.

In spite of being a large winery, the team is still enthused and attentive to the details. "We're not just a factory cranking out product. Our winemaking team is very hands-on and passionate about our craft."

SPICY TURKEY BISCUITS

CHEF: JEFF MAXFIELD, SPACE NEEDLE

MAKES 10

4 oz ground turkey
2 cloves garlic, finely chopped
2 to 3 shiitake mushrooms, stems removed and sliced (¼ cup)
1 carrot, finely chopped or shredded
1 scallion, finely sliced
3 Tbsp Sriracha
2 Tbsp grated ginger
1 Tbsp soy sauce, plus extra for serving
1 Tbsp sesame oil
1 (7.5-oz) can Pillsbury Biscuits dough
Vegetable oil, for greasing
Soy sauce, for dipping

WINE PAIRING: Chateau Ste. Michelle & Dr. Loosen Eroica Riesling

A delicious turkey patty tops a baked biscuit in this super simple recipe, but chicken, pork, and even veggies make favorable substitutes. It's not a dish you might expect to pair with wine, but the spices pair especially well with Chateau Ste. Michelle's Riesling.

In a medium bowl, combine turkey, garlic, mushrooms, carrot, scallion, Sriracha, ginger, soy sauce, and sesame oil.

On a counter, flatten each biscuit to a 3-inch round. Place 1 tablespoon of the mixture on each biscuit, moisten the edges with water, fold over to make a half-moon shape, and pinch the seam to seal. Line a bamboo or metal steamer with a sheet of lightly oiled parchment paper. Place biscuits on the wax paper seam-side up. Cover steamer and steam for 10 minutes, until biscuits reach an internal temperature of 165°F.

Serve with small side dishes of soy sauce for dipping, dim sum style.

HAZELNUT-CRUSTED GOAT CHEESE FRITTERS

with Cabernet-Huckleberry Compote

CHEF: JEFF MAXFIELD, SPACE NEEDLE

Pictured p. 67

SERVES 4

WINE PAIRING: Chateau Ste. Michelle Cold Creek Vineyard Cabernet Sauvignon

This creamy goat cheese fritter makes a great summer starter or light lunch when accompanied with hearty greens. The recipe takes advantage of the wild huckleberries that grow abundantly on our mountainsides in the late summer and early fall, but blackberries or blueberries makes suitable substitutes, too.

Chateau Ste. Michelle's Cabernet Sauvignon makes a reliable pairing. The earthiness of the hazelnuts and huckleberries brings out the dark fruit in this refined wine.

CABERNET-HUCKLEBERRY COMPOTE Combine sugar and lemon juice in a nonreactive saucepan. Add ¼ to ½ cup water to wet the sugar and cook over medium heat until caramelized. Remove from heat and add shallot, star anise, huckleberries (or blackberries), and vinegar. Stir to incorporate. Pour in wine, then return to the heat and cook for another 8 to 10 minutes, until syrupy. Remove from heat and discard star anise. Keep warm.

CABERNET-HUCKLEBERRY COMPOTE

1 cup granulated sugar
Juice of ½ lemon
1 shallot, chopped
1 star anise
¼ cup mountain huckleberries or blackberries
¼ cup red wine vinegar
2 cups Cabernet Sauvignon

GOAT CHEESE FRITTERS

½ lb local chèvre (goat cheese)
1 cup all-purpose flour
3 eggs, beaten
2 cups panko breadcrumbs
1½ cups finely chopped
    toasted and peeled hazelnuts
    (preferably Holmquist
    Hazelnut Orchards)
Vegetable oil, for frying
Finishing salt, to taste

ASSEMBLY

4 cups frisée
1½ Tbsp extra-virgin olive oil
Salt, to taste

GOAT CHEESE FRITTERS Divide cheese into four equal portions. Roll each into a patty about ½ inch thick.

Place flour and eggs into two separate bowls. Combine breadcrumbs and hazelnuts into a third. Coat cheese in flour, then dip it into the egg and dredge it in hazelnut mixture. Place cheese back into the egg and once again into the hazelnut mixture.

Heat an inch of vegetable oil in a saucepan over medium-high heat, until it reaches 340°F (a teaspoon of the hazelnut-panko mixture should brown after 20 to 30 seconds in the oil. If it burns after 10 seconds, the oil is too hot and the heat should be reduced.) Carefully lower cheese into oil and cook for 2 to 3 minutes, until golden brown on one side. Carefully flip it over and brown the other side. Using a slotted spoon, transfer cheese to a wire rack or plate lined with paper towels and season with salt. Keep warm.

ASSEMBLY Combine frisée and oil in a bowl and toss to coat. Season with salt. Place a handful of frisée on each plate and place goat cheese fritter on top, adding compote over half of the fritter. Serve immediately.

COL SOLARE WINERY

+

DAREL ALLWINE

With a surname like Allwine, you'd think the winemaker behind one of Red Mountain's most prominent wineries could have predicted his fate at an early age. But it wasn't until he retired from the U.S. Air Force at the age of thirty-nine that Darel considered wine as a career option. In 1996, he answered a newspaper ad for a cellar worker at Columbia Crest. And once he landed the job, it didn't take him long to fall in love with the industry. "Everything from the vineyards and harvest through to the aging process and bottling fascinated me," says Darel.

Col Solare was started in 1995— in partnership with Chateau Ste. Michelle (page 64) and the Antinori family of Tuscany (among the most successful winemakers in Italy)—with the intent to feature a Bordeaux-style blend that captures the power and concentration of the best Red Mountain Cabernets without the harsh

tannins. "Because the quality of the fruit grown here is so intense and concentrated, you can get a lot of flavor profiles, especially in Bordeaux varietals with an emphasis on Cabernets."

Darel joined Col Solare in 2003, while the project was housed at Columbia Crest. In 2007, Col Solare had its own dedicated winery on Red Mountain. And in 2013, Darel became head winemaker.

What keeps Darel interested in the winemaking business today is the excitement that hooked him in the late 1990s. "Harvest time, for me, is the best time of the year. It's so intense, and I'm at

the winery seven days a week— I wouldn't give that up for anything."

He proves that there's no time like the present to learn about wine, regardless of age. "I was retired when I was introduced to the wine business twenty years ago." And he has never looked back.

ROASTED PORCINI

with Nettle Yogurt, Green Garlic, and Fenugreek-Chili Oil CHEF: LOGAN COX, HOMER

NETTLE YOGURT
2 Tbsp kosher salt, plus extra to taste
½ lb nettles, washed and stems removed
2 cups full-fat yogurt
1 Tbsp honey

ROASTED PORCINI MUSHROOMS
2 lbs large, dense wild porcini or Royal Trumpet mushrooms, cleaned and halved lengthwise
Kosher salt, to taste
¼ cup olive oil
4 cloves garlic, crushed
3 sprigs thyme
2 Tbsp butter

FENUGREEK-CHILI OIL
6 cloves garlic, sliced
1 bay leaf
½ yellow onion, finely chopped
2 Tbsp ground fenugreek
½ tsp Aleppo pepper
½ tsp ground turmeric
¼ cup reserved mushroom oil (see here), room temperature

ASSEMBLY
1 lime
2 bunches green garlic (spring garlic or young garlic), sliced diagonally, for garnish
¼ cup tarragon leaves, for garnish

WINE PAIRING: Col Solare Cabernet Sauvignon

Wild porcinis thrive in vast wooded areas, often under the spruce and pine trees that canopy our state so abundantly. And when these mushrooms are left alone, they grow big—really big. Here, they've been roasted to create a depth of flavor and a mild aroma of cinnamon that pair up well with a rounded red. In this case, Col Solare's Cabernet Sauvignon, with its wild berry and vanilla notes, is our preferred choice.

NETTLE YOGURT Bring a large saucepan of water and salt to a boil. Add nettles and cook for 1 to 2 minutes, until wilted. Transfer nettles to a bowl of ice water. Drain, then squeeze dry.

Chop nettles, then transfer them to a food processor and process for 30 seconds, until finely chopped. Add yogurt and honey and pulse until nettles are evenly distributed. Season with salt, then set aside.

ROASTED PORCINI MUSHROOMS Season mushrooms liberally with salt.

Heat oil in a large skillet over high heat until it begins to smoke. Add mushrooms cut-side down and reduce heat to medium heat. Sear, untouched, for 3 minutes, until it forms a golden-brown crust. Flip mushrooms over, then add garlic, thyme, and butter. Cook for another 2 minutes, basting mushrooms frequently with the butter sauce.

Transfer mushrooms to a plate and keep warm. Strain oil into a small bowl and reserve for the chili oil.

FENUGREEK-CHILI OIL Combine all ingredients in a small saucepan and heat over medium-low heat. Cook for 6 minutes, until garlic is golden brown.

ASSEMBLY Place a small spoon of nettle yogurt on each plate. Place mushrooms on top cut-side up. Drizzle 2 to 3 tablespoons of fenugreek-chili oil on top. Using a Microplane, zest lime on top and garnish with green garlic and tarragon leaves.

PORK CHOPS with Prune
Amba and Chanterelles CHEF: LOGAN COX, HOMER

SERVES 4

WINE PAIRING: Col Solare Cabernet Sauvignon

Amba is a tangy pickle condiment, traditionally made with mango and popular in Indian and Middle Eastern cuisine. Here, it's been given a new flavor profile with sweet, spiced prunes—the key is to prepare it a day in advance to develop the flavors.

Cabernet Sauvignon is seen as an obvious pairing with steaks, but Col Solare's version has a unique profile that goes hand in hand with the complex spices in this dish.

PORK CHOPS Place pork chops on a large baking sheet, spacing them apart. Generously sprinkle salt all over the pork chops and rub it in.

In a spice grinder, combine the remaining ingredients and grind for 30 seconds, until it becomes a fine powder. Transfer mixture to a small bowl and liberally sprinkle the spice mix on the pork chops until evenly coated. Refrigerate, uncovered, overnight.

PRUNE AMBA Heat oil in a large, heavy-bottomed saucepan over medium-high heat until it begins to smoke. Add onion, garlic, chile, and prunes and sauté for 8 minutes, until the onion is lightly caramelized. Add fenugreek, mustard seeds, and cumin and toast for 20 seconds, until fragrant.

Stir in vinegar, 2 cups water, and brown sugar. Cook for 15 to 20 minutes, until mixture is reduced by half and has the consistency of compote. Keep warm. (Leftover prune amba can be stored in an airtight container in the refrigerator for up to a week.)

PORK CHOPS
3 high-quality bone-in pork
  chops, 1 inch thick
Kosher salt
2 bay leaves
3 Tbsp berbere (see Note)
2 Tbsp anise seeds
2 Tbsp ground turmeric
1 tsp urfa biber (see Note)

PRUNE AMBA
½ cup olive oil
1 yellow onion, chopped
8 cloves garlic, sliced
1 ancho chile, soaked, deseeded,
  and chopped
3 cups prunes, chopped
2 tsp ground fenugreek seeds
2 tsp yellow mustard seeds
1 tsp ground cumin seeds
2 cups red wine vinegar
½ cup packed brown sugar

SAUTÉED CHANTERELLES

¼ cup olive oil
5 cloves garlic, thinly sliced
1 shallot, thinly sliced
1 tsp thyme leaves
1 lb chanterelle mushrooms, halved
½ cup chicken stock
3 Tbsp butter
Kosher salt, to taste

ASSEMBLY

Olive oil, for brushing
Frilly mustard greens, torn, for garnish
Mint leaves, torn, for garnish

NOTE: Berbere is an Ethiopian spice blend made with chiles, garlic, ginger, basil, nigella seeds, and korarima (Ethiopian cardamom). Urfa biber is a Turkish chile pepper with a smoky, raisin-like flavor. Both can be found online or at specialty grocers.

SAUTÉED CHANTERELLES Heat oil in a large skillet over medium-high heat until it begins to smoke. Add garlic, shallot, and thyme and sauté for 4 minutes, until garlic is golden. Stir in mushrooms and sauté for another 4 minutes.

Add stock and butter and gently stir for 2 minutes, until liquid has reduced and sauce has emulsified. Season with salt to taste.

ASSEMBLY Preheat grill to high heat. Remove pork chops from the refrigerator and set aside for 25 minutes to bring to room temperature.

Brush pork chops with oil and place them on the grill. Cook for 6 minutes, untouched, until they form a crust. Flip over and cook for another 6 minutes, until the internal temperature reaches 135°F. (If the pork is burning, reduce the heat or move the pork to a cooler part of the grill.)

Transfer pork chops to a plate and set aside to rest for 10 minutes. Using a carving knife, remove the bone from the chops and slice meat into ¼-inch-thick slices.

On a large plate, fan out the pork and spoon chanterelles on top. Add a few dollops of prune amba, then garnish with mustard greens and torn mint leaves.

DAMA WINES

+

MARY DERBY

A classically trained singer, Mary Derby moved to San Francisco in the late 1980s to pursue a career in opera. Like many artists, she waited tables to make ends meet, including stints at the landmark restaurants Stars and Zuni Café, under the tutelage of culinary demigods Jeremiah Tower and Judy Rodgers. "I was like Dorothy from Kansas, walking into Oz from small-town Minnesota. The experience prompted my love of the food and wine community."

In 2000, the family of Mary's late husband, Devin Derby, dangled the ultimate carrot in front of the couple: to move to Walla Walla to start Spring Valley Vineyard (now owned by Ste. Michelle Wine Estates). Without an ounce of winemaking experience, the couple accepted the offer and learned the art of winemaking on the job. When Devin passed away in 2004, Mary took a two-year hiatus from the wine industry. In 2007, she forged ahead and launched DAMA Wines, the name meaning "lady" in Spanish. In 2010, Judith Shulman joined as managing partner.

Mary is best known for her dry and floral Cabernet Franc rosé, which won a gold medal at *Sip* magazine's Best of the Northwest in 2017. "My wines are strong but delicate. I'm looking at vineyards that are producing grapes that are not aggressively tannic monsters." The San Francisco Chronicle Wine Competition has awarded DAMA top prize for their 2014 Cabernet Sauvignon and 2015 Tempranillo, as well as a Double Gold for their 2015 DAMAnation GSM, a blend of Grenache, Syrah, and Mourvèdre.

"As an opera singer, I always sought out the perfect note. The Italian word *squillo* describes the vibration that comes after you stop singing. And the perfect vibration carries on," Mary explains. "I also want that in my wines. That's beauty, that's art."

BROCCOLI with Walnuts, Dried Cherry and Cocoa Nib Gremolata, and Feta
CHEF: ZOI ANTONITSAS

SERVES 2 TO 4

DRIED CHERRY AND COCOA NIB GREMOLATA

½ cup chopped parsley
¼ cup dried cherries, roughly chopped
2 Tbsp cocoa nibs
1 Tbsp chopped marjoram or oregano
Grated zest of 1 orange
Grated zest of 1 lemon
Pinch of salt
Pinch of chili flakes
1 large clove garlic, finely chopped
½ cup extra-virgin olive oil

BROCCOLI

3 Tbsp liquid aminos (preferably Bragg) or tamari
Juice of 1 orange
Juice of 1 lemon
1 Tbsp extra-virgin olive oil
1 tsp smoked paprika (pimentón de la Vera)
1 (2-lb) head broccoli, cut into 1-inch florets
Kosher salt, to taste

ASSSEMBLY

½ cup chopped toasted walnuts
½ cup crumbled feta

WINE PAIRING: DAMA Grenache

This complex and luscious Grenache has notes of cherry, pepper, smoky fruit, tobacco, cedar, and milk chocolate, echoing some of the flavors of this dish. Medium-bodied and silky textured, its character is polished and richly defined.

DRIED CHERRY AND COCOA NIB GREMOLATA In a bowl, combine all ingredients and set aside.

BROCCOLI Preheat grill to high heat. (Alternatively, build a fire in your grill and leave a third of the grill coal-free.)

In a large bowl, whisk together aminos (or tamari), citrus juices, oil, and paprika. Add broccoli and toss to coat. Sprinkle lightly with salt.

Place a grill basket on the grill. Add broccoli and grill for 10 to 12 minutes, tossing frequently, until florets are crisp and edges are charred. If you don't have a grill basket, lay florets out on the grill in a single layer and using tongs, turn them often.

ASSEMBLY Transfer broccoli to a serving platter. Top with walnuts, gremolata, and feta. Serve immediately.

STRAWBERRY SALAD

with Ibérico Ham, Yogurt, Basil, and Marcona Almonds CHEF: ZOI ANTONITSAS

WINE PAIRING: DAMA Rosé

Many people recognize the combination of melon and prosciutto, and this salad is a play on those profiles. It's a crowd-pleaser with an array of savory, sweet, and sour flavors. Chef Zoi Antonitsas prefers local seasonal berries, but even peaches and tomatoes will work well in this salad.

This beautiful and bright Provence-style rosé has flavors of wild strawberry and ruby-grapefruit peel and a salty mineral finish. With a smooth medium body and rich mouthfeel, it begs for summertime, sunshine, and alfresco dining.

In a small bowl, combine shallot, vinegar, salt, and pepper and set aside for 5 minutes. Whisk in oil. (Do not emulsify.)

Put strawberries in a large bowl. Add half of the dressing to the bowl and gently toss. Add arugula and basil and gently toss again. Season with salt and pepper to taste.

Spoon a heaping spoon of yogurt into the center of each plate. Using the back of the spoon, spread the yogurt. Arrange a tall mound of salad in the center. Lay pieces of Ibérico ham (or prosciutto) on top and garnish with almonds and green strawberries and edible flowers, if using. Drizzle extra dressing over each plate. Serve immediately.

1 shallot, finely chopped
1 Tbsp sherry vinegar
¼ tsp kosher salt, plus extra to taste
¼ tsp black pepper, plus extra to taste
2 Tbsp extra-virgin olive oil
1 lb ripe strawberries (about 3 cups), halved lengthwise
2 cups wild arugula
1 cup small green and/or purple basil leaves
¼ cup Greek yogurt (preferably Fage 5% fat)
4 oz Ibérico ham or prosciutto, thinly sliced
¼ cup Marcona almonds, roughly chopped, for garnish
4 green (unripe) strawberries, sliced, for garnish (optional)
Edible flowers, for garnish (optional)

DAMSEL CELLARS

+

MARI WOMACK

After twenty-two years in the restaurant business, Mari Womack wanted to learn how to make wine instead of pouring it for other people. Hers was a circuitous route.

Prior to winemaking, she spent four years at UW and was wait-listed for grad school while working in restaurants to make extra money. Food and drink became the conduit for her future career in the wine business. "You'd have these beautiful pairing menus, and when done correctly, it was mind-blowing."

But it wasn't until years later, in 2010, that she dipped her foot into the pool by volunteering at Obelisco and Baer wineries. "Seeing all the pieces together—the active fermentations, the equipment, and the production side—was an aha moment."

She began making her own wine in 2012 at Darby Winery, where she worked as the assistant winemaker. In 2015, she left the winery, and in 2017, she opened her own facility.

When deciding upon a name, Mari thought that she needed to portray herself as a bombastic, edgy, rock-star winemaker in order to go head to head with her male counterparts. "And the more I thought about it, the more I thought, yeah, that's just not me."

Instead, she did the exact opposite and chose the elegant name Damsel. "I really wanted to have a feminine lean that represented the female side of Washington winemaking," she explains. "Wine can be romantic and feminine, and I like wines with a medium body, nuanced spice, and smoky flavors."

Of course, winemaking needs to be a profitable business. And yes, the product needs to be marketed and sold. But that hasn't ruined the romance for Mari. "I have wonderful days where I can share a bottle of wine and a great meal with friends and know that I've contributed to that experience in a meaningful way. Every now and then I have that moment [of] 'I actually made this!' And that's pretty cool."

CHARRED BABY CARROTS

with Spicy Bacon-Sherry Vinaigrette, Cashew Cream, and Cilantro CHEF AARON TEKULVE, SURRELL

SERVES 4

CASHEW CREAM
1 Tbsp butter
1 large shallot, chopped (¼ cup)
2 cloves garlic, chopped
½ cup half-and-half cream
¼ cup cashews
Grated zest and juice of 1 lime
Salt, to taste

BABY CARROTS WITH BACON-SHERRY VINAIGRETTE
20 to 24 tender young carrots, washed and greens trimmed
¼ cup grapeseed or rice bran oil
1 lb thick-cut smoked bacon (preferably Nueske's Applewood-Smoked Bacon), cut into ½-inch pieces
2 cloves garlic, finely chopped
1 large shallot, finely chopped (¼ cup)
½ serrano chile, deseeded, deveined, and finely chopped (1 Tbsp)
¼ cup sherry vinegar
2 Tbsp wildflower honey
1 Tbsp fish sauce
1 Tbsp aged soy sauce
Salt and black pepper, to taste

ASSEMBLY
1 cup salted cashews, toasted and roughly chopped, for garnish
1 cup chopped cilantro, for garnish

WINE PAIRING: Damsel Cabernet Sauvignon

Chef Aaron Tekulve proves that even the humblest vegetable can be exciting to eat, and he loves to prepare this dish in fall when carrots are sweeter. A gutsy smoky char adds depth and helps to cinch the flavors together with Damsel's smoky, herbaceous wine infused with subtle notes of dried cherry.

CASHEW CREAM Heat butter in a saucepan over medium heat. Add shallot and garlic and sauté for 2 to 3 minutes, until softened. (Do not caramelize.) Add cream and cashews, then reduce heat to medium-low and simmer for 7 to 10 minutes, until cashews have softened.

Transfer mixture to a blender and purée, until mixture is smooth and has a yogurt-like consistency. (If necessary, add a little water.) Add lime zest and juice, then season to taste with salt. Set aside. (Makes about 1 cup.)

BABY CARROTS WITH BACON-SHERRY VINAIGRETTE
Preheat broiler to high heat. Place rack on the top shelf.

In a large bowl, combine carrots and oil and toss well. Place carrots in a single layer on a baking sheet and broil for 5 to 7 minutes on each side, until blackened and tender. They should be cooked through but still have a bite to them. (If needed, roast at 400°F for another 3 to 5 minutes.) Set aside to cool.

Heat a skillet over medium heat. Add bacon and cook for 5 to 7 minutes, until crisp and golden. Turn off heat, then add garlic, shallot, and chile and sauté for 10 to 20 seconds. Add vinegar, honey, fish sauce, and soy sauce and stir well.

Transfer carrots to large bowl and pour in bacon-sherry vinaigrette. Mix well, then season with salt and pepper. Keep warm.

ASSEMBLY Place a smear of cashew cream on four plates. Arrange five to six carrots on each plate, then drizzle with vinaigrette. Garnish with cashews and cilantro.

ROASTED SWEET POTATO AND CURRY SOUP with

Apple-Cilantro Salsa and Yogurt

CHEF: AARON TEKULVE, SURRELL

APPLE-CILANTRO SALSA

1 Honeycrisp apple, cored and
  cut into ¼-inch cubes
1 large clove garlic, finely chopped
1 (1-inch) knob ginger, peeled and
  grated
½ bunch cilantro, leaves and
  stems, finely chopped
1 tsp finely chopped shallot
½ tsp finely chopped serrano
  chile
¼ cup extra-virgin olive oil
Grated zest and juice of 1 lime,
  plus extra if needed
Salt, to taste

GREEK YOGURT SAUCE

⅓ cup Greek yogurt
1 Tbsp extra-virgin olive oil
Salt and black pepper, to taste
Smoking gun (optional)

ROASTED SWEET POTATO AND CURRY SOUP

3 Tbsp rendered beef fat or
  butter
2 Tbsp butter
4 shallots, chopped (1 cup)
4 cloves garlic, chopped
2 Tbsp chopped ginger
4 to 6 sweet potatoes, peeled
  and cut into chunks (4 cups)
2 Tbsp yellow curry powder
2 Tbsp red miso paste
½ cup white wine
4 cups chicken stock, plus extra
  if needed
1 bay leaf
½ cup heavy cream
¼ cup sherry vinegar, plus extra
  to taste
1 to 2 Tbsp high-quality soy sauce
1 Tbsp fish sauce
Salt and black pepper, to taste

WINE PAIRING: Damsel The Fates GSM

This soup is a great expression of Aaron Tekulve's cooking style: it's deceptively simple yet supported with deep flavors and strong techniques. If you're looking to go all out, use a smoking gun to smoke the yogurt sauce and give it a depth of flavor and interest that will elevate the soup.

Damsel's classy wine has a seamless texture, a balanced and elegant finish, and a boldness and acidity level to complement the soup. The wine's toasted spice flavors work well with the curry.

APPLE-CILANTRO SALSA In a bowl, combine all ingredients and mix well. Season to taste with salt and more lime. Set aside. (Makes 1 cup.)

GREEK YOGURT SAUCE In a small bowl, combine yogurt, oil, and salt and pepper. Add 1 to 2 tablespoons water to thin out the mixture. The sauce should be thin enough to coat the back of a spoon and drizzle over the soup. If desired, smoke the yogurt with your smoking gun. Refrigerate until needed. (Makes ½ cup.)

ROASTED SWEET POTATO AND CURRY SOUP Heat beef fat and butter in a stockpot over medium heat until lightly browned. Add shallot, garlic, and ginger and sauté for 3 to 5 minutes, until softened and fragrant. Add sweet potatoes, curry powder, and miso and mix well. Pour in wine and cook for another 3 to 5 minutes, until slightly reduced.

Add stock and bay leaf and cook for 20 to 30 minutes, until sweet potatoes are very soft. Discard bay leaf and add heavy cream, vinegar, soy sauce, and fish sauce. Transfer soup, in batches, to a blender and purée until smooth. The soup should have the consistency of thick cream. (If necessary, add more stock.) Season with salt and pepper.

Ladle soup into bowls and garnish with apple-cilantro salsa and a drizzle of Greek yogurt sauce.

DOUBLEBACK
WINERY

+

JOSH
MCDANIELS

As one of the youngest winemakers in the region, Josh McDaniels may not have the storied tales of some of his seasoned peers, but he certainly has his own unique spin on the industry.

Josh, who's barely into his thirties, was born and raised in Walla Walla. And while that suggests that he was brought into this world with a propensity toward grapes, he actually fell in love with the business way before the product. While working at Leonetti Cellar one day in 2007, Josh met his hometown hero: the former New England Patriots quarterback Drew Bledsoe. "[When I was] growing up in Walla Walla, Drew was like a mythical godlike figure for every young boy," says Josh. So what did he do? Josh helped Drew realize his dream of helming an estate-run winery with a focus on exceptional Cabernet Sauvignon.

In 2014, Josh was hired on as head winemaker of Doubleback, a nod to Drew's return or "doubling back" to his hometown of Walla Walla. The wines are styled after those in the Old World: less alcohol and more balanced oak composition and natural acidity. It's the type of wine Drew has always enjoyed.

"Drew retired from a competitive job at an early age, and I had something to prove," says Josh. "We work well together because we're both competitive with high standards."

> Wagyu Rib-Eye Steak with Basque-Style Potatoes and Charred Eggplant Black Garlic Purée | p. 86

WAGYU RIB-EYE STEAK

with Basque-Style Potatoes and Charred Eggplant Black Garlic Purée CHEF: SHAWN APPLIN, RN74

Pictured p. 85

SERVES 4

WINE PAIRING: Doubleback Estate Reserve Cabernet Sauvignon

Steak and potatoes are a match made in heaven, but the charred eggplant and black garlic purée—savory, smoky, and sweet all at once—makes a decidedly sophisticated and suitable accompaniment when serving this dish in late spring or summer. Pair it with this elegant, full-bodied Cabernet Sauvignon, which rises to the occasion.

WAGYU RIB-EYE STEAK In a bowl, combine Espelette pepper, pepper, salt, and oil. Spread paste over the steak. Cover and refrigerate overnight.

PICKLED MUSTARD SEEDS In a large saucepan, bring 2 quarts of water to a boil. Add mustard seeds and blanch for 3 minutes. Drain. Repeat two more times, discarding the water each time.

In a small saucepan, combine vinegar, salt, sugar, and ½ cup water and bring to a boil. Add mustard seeds to the pickling liquid and set aside for at least 24 hours.

CHARRED EGGPLANT PURÉE Preheat grill or broiler to high heat.

Pierce eggplant a few times for venting. Place eggplant on the grill or in the oven and roast for 20 to 30 minutes, turning occasionally, until it is completely charred, soft on the inside, and collapses on itself. Set aside to cool.

Trim off top of eggplant, then transfer it, with skin and juices, into a blender. Add black garlic, oil, vinegar, honey, and salt and purée on high speed. Keep warm.

WAGYU RIB-EYE STEAK
3 Tbsp Espelette pepper
2 Tbsp black pepper
1 Tbsp kosher salt
6 Tbsp olive oil
4 (14- to 16-oz) wagyu rib-eye or good-quality steaks

PICKLED MUSTARD SEEDS
½ cup yellow mustard seeds
2 cups rice vinegar
2 Tbsp kosher salt
2 Tbsp granulated sugar

CHARRED EGGPLANT PURÉE
1 eggplant
1 head black garlic (see Note)
1 cup olive oil
6 Tbsp sherry vinegar
2 Tbsp honey
1 Tbsp kosher salt

BASQUE-STYLE POTATOES
1 lb marble-colored new
   potatoes
1 cup kosher salt

ASSEMBLY
Small mustard greens, for garnish

> **NOTE:** Black garlic can
> be purchased in Asian
> food markets, but you
> can also make your
> own. Place heads of
> garlic in a rice cooker
> or slow cooker on the
> "keep warm" setting
> and slowly cook for
> 14 days.

BASQUE-STYLE POTATOES In a large saucepan, combine potatoes, salt, and 2 quarts cold water and bring to a boil. Cook potatoes for 10 minutes, until tender. (The potatoes will be very salty, and the skin will turn white.) Drain, then transfer to a baking sheet to cool. (This will allow the salt to set on the outside of the potato, creating a layer of white salt.) Set aside for at least 5 minutes.

ASSEMBLY Preheat a charcoal or gas grill to high heat.

Grill steaks over medium-high heat for 8 to 10 minutes on each side for medium-rare (or until it reaches an internal temperature of 120°F). Transfer to a plate and set aside for 5 to 8 minutes to rest.

If needed, warm the potatoes in the oven. Heat the eggplant purée just until it's hot. Spoon the purée onto warm plates, then add steaks. Add potatoes. Drizzle pickled mustard seeds on the steak and garnish with mustard greens. Serve immediately.

IBÉRICO PORK STRIPLOIN

with Roasted Shallot Saffron Purée, Hazelnut Chimichurri, and Grilled Asparagus CHEF: SHAWN APPLIN, RN74

WINE PAIRING: Doubleback Cabernet Sauvignon

The Ibérico breed of pig, which is native to Spain and feeds off a special diet of acorns, has a superb nutty flavor. High-quality pork doesn't demand long cooking times; in fact, chef Shawn Applin prefers to cook this succulent striploin to medium-rare. If Ibérico is unavailable, look for a young milk- or nut-fed breed.

This breed is high in fat, so it demands a wine that is rich, robust, and with huge tannins. Doubleback's Cabernet Sauvignon meets the challenge: it has explosive notes of berries and a hint of allspice, a luscious palate, and a long, dramatic finish that serves this dish well.

PORK STRIPLOIN In a large bowl, combine oil, garlic, and rosemary and thyme sprigs. Season with salt and pepper. Put steaks in the bowl and coat in marinade. Set aside at room temperature for 1 hour.

SHALLOT PURÉE Preheat oven to 350°F.

In a deep casserole dish, combine whole shallots, garlic, and oil. Cover with aluminum foil and roast for 12 to 15 minutes, until the shallots are very soft and slightly browned. Set aside to cool.

Transfer mixture to a blender. Add hazelnuts, almonds, saffron, and salt and pepper and purée until smooth. (If needed, add a little more oil to loosen mixture.) Set aside.

PORK STRIPLOIN

1 cup extra-virgin olive oil
4 cloves garlic, chopped
Bunch of rosemary
½ bunch thyme
Salt and black pepper, to taste
1 (1 lb) Ibérico pork striploin, divided into 4 steaks and trimmed of sinew

SHALLOT PURÉE

3 shallots, peeled
2 cloves garlic
1 cup olive oil, plus extra if needed
½ cup peeled or blanched hazelnuts
¼ cup Marcona almonds
½ Tbsp saffron threads
Salt and black pepper, to taste

HAZELNUT CHIMICHURRI

1 cup hazelnuts, blanched or
   peeled after toasting
2 bunches parsley, finely chopped
½ cup finely chopped garlic
2 cups extra-virgin olive oil
½ cup sherry vinegar
Salt and black pepper, to taste

ASSEMBLY

Asparagus, trimmed
Miner's lettuce, for garnish
Finishing salt and black pepper,
   to taste

HAZELNUT CHIMICHURRI Preheat oven to 350°F.

Spread out hazelnuts in a single layer on a baking sheet and toast for 12 minutes, until fragrant. Set aside to cool.

Put hazelnuts into a food processor or blender and process until fine. Transfer hazelnuts to a bowl, add parsley, garlic, oil, and vinegar, and mix well. Season with salt and pepper. Set aside.

ASSEMBLY Preheat grill to high heat (400°F).

Add pork and grill for 12 to 15 minutes for medium-rare, until internal temperature reaches 120°F. Set aside.

Grill the asparagus for 4 to 6 minutes, until slightly charred. Spread shallot purée on each plate. Slice pork and fan out over the purée. Drizzle chimichurri on top and garnish with lettuce. Season with salt and pepper.

FIELDING HILLS WINERY

+

MIKE WADE

When was the last time a glass of cheap house wine from a local diner changed your life? For Mike Wade, it was around 1979.

Mike, who was a business major at the University of Washington, comes from a multigenerational agriculture family. His grandfather arrived in Wenatchee in 1921 and started a cherry business, which Mike's father joined in the early 1950s. After graduating from college, Mike returned to Wenatchee as the third generation in the family business.

"The Chieftain restaurant, which is no longer there, was my grandmother's favorite spot," Mike reminisces. "I remember ordering prime rib and accompanying it with a glass of house Burgundy. The steak with the horseradish and the jus was delicious—then I had a sip of the wine and

thought, 'Wow!'" What seemed like an ordinary dining experience became a revelatory moment that shaped Mike's career path.

Mike and his wife, Karen, inspired by a passion for great wine, started Fielding Hills Winery in 2000. For the first thirteen years, they produced wine in a tractor shed located in East Wenatchee, on an orchard where they still live. "Mike sent a wine to *Wine Spectator*, and our first vintage, a 2000 Cabernet Sauvignon, received ninety-one points from two-year-old vines," says Karen. "That's when the phone started ringing." *Wine Spectator* soon named Mike the "rising star" winemaker of Washington state.

In order to meet increasing demand for their wine, the couple ultimately moved out of the tractor shed and opened a beautiful production facility and tasting room on Lake Chelan. "We have a great team," says Mike, who is still CEO of the family apple and cherry business. And with the move to Lake Chelan, winemaker Tyler Armour has stepped up to create the daily vision that follows Mike's core values of producing world-class wines.

> *Pork Belly Lettuce Wraps* | p. 92

PORK BELLY LETTUCE WRAPS CHEF: DEREK SIMCIK

Pictured p. 91

SERVES 8

WINE PAIRING: Fielding Hills Old Vine Chenin Blanc

Pork belly is fattier than most cuts, which can be advantageous when the fat renders off and leaves the meat succulent and full of flavor. And because the pork is served with kimchi apples, pickled scallions, and scallion chermoula in a lettuce wrap, the final dish is fresh, balanced, and surprisingly light. Be sure to prepare this dish well in advance: the pork requires 48 hours of brining.

Oh, but the payoff is worth your while. The combination of sweetness and fattiness showcases the strength of Fielding Hills Winery's dry Chenin Blanc, boasting crisp apple and herbaceous aromas.

BRINED PORK In a large saucepan, combine vinegar, brown sugar, salt, thyme, and 6 cups of water. Stir and simmer until the sugar and salt dissolve. Pour mixture into a large glass bowl and add 3 to 4 cups of ice to cool down and dilute the brine. Add belly to brine and refrigerate for 48 hours.

KIMCHI APPLES Cut the apples, skin intact, into ⅛-inch-thick slices. Cut the slices into ½-inch-wide strips. (An efficient way to do this is on a mandoline in one move, using the wide julienne blade attachment.)

Combine all ingredients in a bowl and using your hands, toss thoroughly. Adjust seasoning to taste. Refrigerate, covered, until needed.

PICKLED SCALLION In a small saucepan, combine all ingredients except the scallion. Add ¼ cup water and bring to a boil. Reduce heat to medium and simmer for 5 minutes. Add scallion and cook for 5 minutes, stirring occasionally, until onion is slightly translucent.

Remove pan from heat and transfer scallion into a mason jar. Pour in liquid on top. Cover tightly and refrigerate the jar on its side until needed.

BRINED PORK
¼ cup apple cider vinegar
¼ cup packed brown sugar
2 Tbsp kosher salt
1 tsp dried thyme
1 (5- to 8-lb) pork belly

KIMCHI APPLES
2 green apples, cored
1 (1-inch) knob ginger, peeled and grated
1 to 2 Tbsp soy sauce
1 Tbsp rice vinegar
1 to 2 Tbsp gochugaru (Korean chili powder)
1 tsp granulated sugar
¼ tsp sesame oil

PICKLED SCALLION
¾ cup apple cider vinegar
6 Tbsp granulated sugar
1 tsp sea salt
1 tsp mustard seeds
1 tsp celery seeds
4 to 6 scallions, white and light green parts only (dark green tops reserved), kept whole

SCALLION CHERMOULA

1 cup packed parsley leaves
1 cup packed cilantro leaves and
   stems
4 to 6 reserved scallion tops
1 clove garlic
¾ tsp kosher salt, plus extra to
   taste
¼ tsp ground cumin
Pinch of ground cinnamon
Large pinch of Aleppo pepper or
   chili flakes
Grated zest of 1 lemon
¾ cup extra-virgin olive oil, plus
   extra if needed
2 Tbsp red wine vinegar

LETTUCE WRAPS

Bibb lettuce or any other leafy
   lettuce, leaves separated
Kimchi Apples (see here)
Scallion Chermoula (see here)
Pickled Scallions (see here)

SCALLION CHERMOULA In a blender, combine all ingredients except the oil and vinegar, and purée. With the motor running, gradually add oil in a steady stream, stopping once or twice to scrape down the sides. Pulse in vinegar. The chermoula should be loose enough to drizzle. Add more oil if needed. Adjust seasoning to taste.

LETTUCE WRAPS Preheat oven to 450°F.

Remove belly from brine and place in a roasting pan fat-side up. Cook belly for 1 hour, until golden brown. Reduce temperature to 250°F and cook for another 1 hour to 1 hour 15 minutes, until the belly is tender but not falling apart. Remove the pan from the oven and transfer belly to a plate. Set aside to cool, then refrigerate until fully chilled and firm.

When it's time to serve, preheat oven to 250°F. Return belly to oven for 10 minutes, until skin turns crispy.

Slice pork belly and place on a board or plate. Arrange lettuce leaves and small bowls of the accompaniments around the board. Allow guests to build their wraps.

"BBQ" QUAIL with Baked Beans
and Pickled Apricots CHEF: DEREK SIMCIK

WINE PAIRING: Fielding Hills Cabernet Sauvignon

Served at Conversation in the Thompson hotel, this BBQ quail is a riff on southern BBQ chicken with baked beans. However, this version features baked beans inspired by a secret recipe from the chef's mother.

The quail stuffing highlights the already pronounced cherry notes in Fielding Hills' Cabernet Sauvignon, while subtle flavors of baking spices and cocoa may also be detected.

PICKLED APRICOTS Sterilize a few 8-ounce canning jars.

Bring a large saucepan of water to a boil. Fill a large bowl with ice water. Carefully lower apricots into boiling water and blanch for 30 to 60 seconds. Using a slotted spoon, transfer apricots to the bowl of ice water and set aside until cool enough to handle.

Remove skins. Cut each apricot in half and remove pit. Cut each half in half to make quarters. Pack apricots into the jars, leaving a ½-inch headspace.

In a heavy-bottomed saucepan, combine the remaining ingredients. Bring to a boil, then reduce heat to medium-low and simmer, uncovered, for 5 minutes, until syrupy. Remove from heat. Pour liquid over apricots. Set aside for 30 minutes.

Gently tap jars on the countertop to remove any air bubbles. Wipe jar rims. Seal with lids. Let sit overnight.

BAKED BEANS Soak beans in a large bowl of water overnight or for at least 6 hours.

Strain beans and place them in a large Dutch oven with a tight-fitting lid. Add salt and pour in enough cool water to cover the beans by 2 inches. Bring to a boil, then reduce heat to medium-low and gently simmer for 30 to 40 minutes, stirring occasionally, until beans are just tender. Drain and remove beans.

PICKLED APRICOTS
2 lbs ripe apricots
1 cup white balsamic vinegar
½ cup sweet vermouth
½ cup raw sugar
2 Tbsp yellow mustard seeds

BAKED BEANS
2 cups dried cranberry beans
1 tsp kosher salt, plus extra
 to taste
3 Tbsp olive oil
1 onion, chopped
⅓ cup molasses
2 tsp dry mustard
2 tsp Worcestershire sauce
1 tsp black pepper

NOTE: Grains of paradise, also known as melegueta pepper, is a spice mostly grown on the western coast of Africa. The small reddish-brown seeds have a peppery yet fruity flavor. Isomalt is more resistant to humidity and crystallization than regular sugar, giving the glaze an extra shine. Both can be purchased online or at specialty grocers.

BBQ GLAZE

1 Tbsp raw sugar
2½ tsp hot paprika
½ Tbsp nigella seeds
½ Tbsp ground cumin
½ Tbsp grains of paradise (see Note) or cardamom
1¼ tsp onion powder
1 tsp celery seeds
1 tsp Espelette pepper
1 tsp dry mustard
1 tsp granulated garlic
1 tsp kosher salt
1 tsp black pepper
1½ Tbsp isomalt (see Note) or granulated sugar
½ cup (1 stick) butter, cut into ½-inch cubes

"BBQ" QUAIL

2 oz ground pork
2 cloves garlic, finely chopped
2½ Tbsp panko breadcrumbs
Salt and black pepper, to taste
8 (12-oz) quails
Melted butter, for brushing

ASSEMBLY

Small handful of mustard greens, for garnish

Preheat oven to 250°F. Bring water to a boil in a kettle or saucepan.

Heat oil in the Dutch oven over medium-high heat. Add onion and cook for 3 to 4 minutes, until it begins to brown.

In a small bowl, combine molasses, mustard, Worcestershire sauce, and pepper. Add this mixture to the pan of onions, then stir in beans. Add enough boiling water to cover beans. Cover and bake for 4 to 5 hours, until they are tender but not falling apart. (Add more water, if needed, to make sure beans are always covered.)

Remove beans from oven, stir, and season with salt. Return pot to oven, uncovered, and cook for another 45 minutes, until the sauce has thickened and the surface is crusty.

BBQ GLAZE In a spice grinder, combine all ingredients except the isomalt (or sugar) and butter and grind to a fine powder.

In a small saucepan, combine isomalt and 2 tablespoons of water and cook over medium heat for 5 minutes, until liquid is almost entirely reduced. Add butter and mix well. Whisk in spice mix and set aside.

"BBQ" QUAIL Preheat broiler.

In a bowl, combine pork, garlic, panko, and salt and pepper. Separate the skin from the breast of each quail, and stuff with equal amounts of the stuffing mixture. Arrange the quail in a baking dish and brush with melted butter.

Broil quail for 7 minutes. Turn over and broil for another 7 minutes, until they reach an internal temperature of 185°F.

ASSEMBLY Place a couple of spoonfuls of baked beans onto each plate. Place quail in the center of beans. Brush BBQ glaze over each quail, then drizzle a small amount around beans. Add pickled apricots and mustard greens, then serve.

FRICHETTE WINERY

+

GREG AND SHAE FRICHETTE

When Shae and Greg Frichette decided they wanted to settle down, they were determined to move closer to their families. But whose side? Shae's family lived in South Carolina, and Greg's were in the Tri-Cities. So they flipped a coin, and Greg won.

"If we were going to move to Washington, we wanted to do something that would give us goosebumps," says Shae. They just didn't know what that was. "Most of the time we were dreaming, we were drinking wine. And just like that, I wondered, why not wine?"

Soon after, Greg enrolled in the enology program at WSU, and the following year in 2011, the couple began hunting for property on Red Mountain. By 2013, they moved north and opened their winery.

The couple fell in love with Bordeaux varieties, which grow well on Red Mountain. And Frichette wines do a great job showcasing the concentrated fruit characteristics and intense flavor of the grapes from the region. "Smoothness and easy tannins make our wines unique," says Shae. "Every wine from our Cabernet Sauvignon to our reserve blends is full of flavor and nicely balanced with fruit and oak."

Settled in their life on Red Mountain, Shae and Greg are on the right path. "When we first began producing wine, it felt like the initial stages of dating someone you really like—when you're completely smitten and obsess over the other person. Now, we're in the been-married-eleven-years stage [and it may be less exciting], but our expectations are greater because we've put in the work."

SMOKED BLACK COD CROSTINI

CHEF: BRIAN CLEVENGER, GENERAL HARVEST RESTAURANTS

SERVES 4
(AS AN APPETIZER)

AIOLI
1 egg
1 egg yolk
1 Tbsp Dijon mustard
Grated zest and juice of 1 lemon
1 cup canola oil
Salt and black pepper, to taste

SMOKED BLACK COD CROSTINI
1 Tbsp kosher salt, plus extra
   to taste
1 tsp black pepper, plus extra
   to taste
1 tsp granulated sugar
1 lb fresh skinless black cod or
   salmon fillets
Applewood or maple wood chips,
   for smoking
1 baguette, cut into ¾-inch-thick
   slices
Extra-virgin olive oil, for brushing
1 cup Aioli (see here)
Grated zest and juice of 1 small
   lemon
Pickled vegetables, for garnish
   (optional)
Chopped chives, for garnish
   (optional)

WINE PAIRING: Frichette Sémillon

Black cod, or sablefish, is a mild white fish from the northern Pacific Ocean with a high fat content and rich, buttery, melt-in-your-mouth texture that is enhanced when smoked. This dish is easy to make and absolutely delicious, but you will need a smoker. (You can also purchase quality smoked sable at finer grocers.)

The green apple and citrus notes in the Frichette Sémillon pair really well with seafood, especially with the introduction of smoke.

AIOLI In a blender or food processor, combine egg, egg yolk, mustard, lemon zest and juice, and 1 tablespoon cold water. With the motor running, gradually add oil and blend until emulsified. Season with salt and pepper. Cool in refrigerator until needed.

SMOKED BLACK COD CROSTINI In a small bowl, combine salt, pepper, and sugar. Season cod (or salmon) with the mixture, then wrap in plastic and refrigerate overnight.

Preheat a smoker to 165°F. Place wood chips in the smoker and add cod. Cook for 20 to 25 minutes, until the cod reaches an internal temperature of 160°F. Remove cod from heat and cool. Chill in the refrigerator.

Preheat grill or oven to 400°F.

Brush baguette with oil, then season with salt and pepper. If using an oven, place on a baking sheet. Grill or toast for 3 minutes on each side.

Cut the chilled cod into large chunks. In a bowl, combine cod, aioli, and lemon zest and juice. Season with salt and pepper.

Serve cod mixture on top of baguette and garnish with pickled vegetables and chives, if using.

BITTER GREENS SALAD, CHERRIES, WALNUTS, AND BALSAMIC VINAIGRETTE

CHEF: BRIAN CLEVENGER, GENERAL HARVEST RESTAURANTS

BALSAMIC VINAIGRETTE
½ cup balsamic vinegar
1 egg
1 egg yolk
1 Tbsp Dijon mustard
1½ cups canola oil
Salt, to taste

SALAD
2 heads frisée, chopped
1 radicchio, chopped
1 Belgian endive, chopped
2 cups arugula
1 tsp kosher salt, plus extra
   to taste
Black pepper, to taste
⅔ cup Balsamic Vinaigrette
   (see here, divided)
1 cup cherries, pitted
¾ cup shaved Parmesan, plus
   extra for garnish
¼ cup chopped toasted walnuts

WINE PAIRING: Frichette Reserve Blend

Bitter greens—such as frisée, radicchio, and endive—add texture and excitement to salads, especially when these nutrient-rich leaves are paired with balsamic vinaigrette and candied nuts. The Reserve Blend makes a fine companion, dazzling with aromas of dark cherry, vanilla, and bramble-berry, firm yet well-integrated tannins, and a silky-smooth texture.

BALSAMIC VINAIGRETTE In food processor or blender, combine balsamic vinegar, egg, egg yolk, and mustard and mix well. With the motor running, gradually add oil in a steady stream until emulsified. Season with salt and set aside. (Leftover vinaigrette can be stored in the refrigerator for up to 2 days.)

SALAD In a large bowl, combine frisée, radicchio, endive, and arugula. Add salt, pepper, ⅓ cup of the vinaigrette, cherries, Parmesan, and walnuts. Mix well. Add more vinai-grette, if needed. Place on large serving platter and garnish with more Parmesan.

GOOSE RIDGE ESTATE VINEYARD & WINERY

+

ANDREW WILSON

Launched in 1998, Goose Ridge Estate Vineyard & Winery is built on acreage pioneered by M.L. Monson and his family in the early 1900s. Thanks to Monson's visionary son Arvid, what was once land intended for cattle and orchards is now considered the largest contiguous estate vineyard in Washington. Now led by Arvid's three children—Bill, Molly, and Valerie—the estate produces grapes for five labels, including Goose Ridge, g3, Tall Sage, StoneCap, and Cascadian Outfitters.

"The challenge is in finding more ways to layer different characteristics and flavors into several wines that are produced with grapes from a single site," says Andrew Wilson, who joined Goose Ridge as head winemaker in 2014.

Andrew studied engineering at Georgia Tech but enrolled in Walla Walla Community College's viticulture and enology program in 2004 after becoming interested in the science, farming, and craft of the Washington wine industry. "One never really stops learning about wine—there will always be winemakers and viticulturists who approach things differently."

His first winery jobs were at the prestigious Forgeron and Long Shadows, working with veteran winemakers Marie-Eve Gilla and Gilles Nicault. "I was fortunate enough to work with some talented winemakers."

Goose Ridge is dedicated to handcrafting limited-production Bordeaux and Rhône varieties, defined by estate-grown grapes.

"I make sure that my winemaking process doesn't mask the unique qualities of the vineyard sites." The flagship Vireo red blend is a good example. "It's always equal parts Cabernet, Merlot, and Syrah, so you can see individual characteristics from each of those varieties."

PAN-ROASTED RAINBOW
TROUT with Beurre Blanc

CHEF: BREANNA BEIKE, HERITAGE RESTAURANT | BAR

BEURRE BLANC
¾ cup (1½ sticks) cold good-
  quality butter (preferably
  Plugrá), cubed (divided)
1 shallot, finely chopped (¼ cup)
Sprig of thyme, leaves only,
  chopped
3 Tbsp white wine vinegar
2 Tbsp dry white wine
½ cup heavy cream
Salt, to taste

PAN-ROASTED RAINBOW TROUT
1 cup almond flour
2 (9- to 11-oz) whole rainbow
  trout, butterflied (ask your
  fishmonger to do this)
Salt and black pepper, to taste
3 Tbsp canola oil
2 Tbsp butter
½ shallot, finely chopped
3 cloves garlic, finely chopped
2 to 3 slices bacon, chopped
  (½ cup)
2 cups prepared tri-color quinoa,
  cooked in vegetable stock
2 cups chopped Swiss chard
½ cup white wine

ASSEMBLY
½ cup demi-glace (see Note)
½ cup Beurre Blanc (see here)
½ cup Marcona almonds,
  chopped, for garnish (optional)
¼ bunch parsley, chopped, for
  garnish (optional)

NOTE: Demi-glace
(veal glaze) can be
found at fine food
stores. Alternatively,
use a premium beef
base (located in the
soup and stock aisle
of supermarkets) and
thicken with a little
cornstarch.

WINE PAIRING: Goose Ridge Sol Duc Meritage

When Heritage first opened in Woodinville, chef Breanna
Beike created this signature dish. The almond flour makes this
dish naturally gluten-free, but you can, of course, substitute a
different flour.

Serve this dish with Goose Ridge's 2014 Sol Duc—the
smokiness of the bacon and toasted almond notes of the fish
will mesh well with the dark fruit and spiced flavors in this wine.

BEURRE BLANC Heat 2 tablespoons butter in a saucepan
over medium heat. Add shallot and thyme and sauté for
2 to 3 minutes. Add vinegar and wine and cook for another
8 to 10 minutes, until reduced by half.

Add cream and salt and bring to a boil. Reduce heat to
low and add the remaining butter, a few cubes at a time,
whisking rapidly. Strain sauce through a fine-mesh strainer.
Keep warm.

PAN-ROASTED RAINBOW TROUT Place almond flour in
a shallow pan. Season the inside of the trout with salt and
pepper, then add fish flesh-side down in the flour.

Heat oil a large skillet or griddle over medium-high heat,
tilting pan to evenly coat surface. Add trout flesh-side down
and cook for 3 minutes, until flour is golden brown. Flip the
fish. Cook for another 3 minutes. Set aside.

Heat butter in another skillet over medium heat for
2 minutes, until bubbly. Add shallot, garlic, and bacon and
sauté for 3 minutes, until bacon begins to caramelize. Add
quinoa and Swiss chard, then stir.

Add wine and cook for another 3 minutes, until mixture
is heated. Season with salt and pepper to taste.

ASSEMBLY Transfer quinoa mixture to a large platter.
Arrange the almond-crusted trout on top. Drizzle warm
demi-glace and beurre blanc over the fish. Garnish with
almonds and parsley, if using.

SPICY CLAMS with Chorizo

CHEF: BREANNA BEIKE, HERITAGE RESTAURANT | BAR

SERVES 4

WINE PAIRING: Goose Ridge Syrah

Clams team up with spicy chorizo in this super-simple and delicious Spanish dish that is served with crusty bread to sop up juices. Be sure to use quality clams such as those from Hama Hama Company, who are committed to quality and sustainability.

The Goose Ridge Syrah has pepper notes that blend nicely with the chorizo and spicy undertones of the broth.

In a small skillet over medium heat, crumble in the chorizo and cook until it no longer looks raw. Drain the chorizo and set aside.

Heat 2 tablespoons butter in a large skillet over medium-high heat. Add onion, shallot, garlic, peppers, and drained chorizo and cook for 7 minutes, until onion is softened. Add clams, chili flakes, tomato sauce, and wine. Cover and steam for 4 to 5 minutes, until clams are halfway open. Add the remaining 2 tablespoons butter and cilantro. Continue to steam for another 4 to 5 minutes, until clams are fully open. Discard any unopened clams. Season with salt and pepper.

Ladle into bowls. Serve immediately with crusty bread.

4 oz fresh Mexican chorizo
¼ cup (½ stick) butter (divided)
1 white onion, thinly sliced
   (½ cup)
1 small shallot, finely chopped
6 cloves garlic, finely chopped
½ cup chopped roasted red
   peppers
1 lb Manila clams, cleaned
2 tsp chili flakes
1 cup tomato sauce
½ cup dry white wine
1 Tbsp chopped cilantro
Salt and black pepper, to taste
Crusty bread, to serve

GORMAN WINERY

+

CHRIS GORMAN

When Chris Gorman found himself following his band (he's the guitarist) from Bellingham down to Seattle after college, a new path unveiled itself. He landed a job as the warehouse manager at a small wine distributor and took an immediate interest. And while he had never drunk a bottle of wine prior to that, he was on the fast track to appreciating wines and secured a similar role at a much larger distributor. It would be the last paid job he'd have before opening his own winery.

Since 2002, Gorman Winery has been producing bold, showy wines that are aggressive, flavored, and full of structure. "I very much have a consumer palate, and as a result, our wines speak to a broad audience," he shares. "My wines don't need to accompany a meal; they should be part of the meal." He likes to make unapologetic wines that buck trends. "We just want to make something that is delicious."

The names of his wines are caricatures of the grapes used: the Bully is a strong-shouldered Cabernet made with Red Mountain grapes, while the Big Sissy is a very malleable Chardonnay that can take a beating. "We had a wine called the Cry Baby, which was named after our cryogenically frozen ice wine. Evil Twin is a combination of Syrah and Cabernet, the two grapes that we do."

High-quality ingredients are pervasive in both the wine and chef communities, and approach to the final product is also similar. "Chefs want to wow you and give you a reason to return. It's the same with winemakers."

> Charred Octopus, Hazelnut Romesco, Broccolini, and Sherry Gastrique | p. 106

CHARRED OCTOPUS,

Hazelnut Romesco, Broccolini, and Sherry Gastrique CHEF: CAROLYNN SPENCE, SHAKER + SPEAR

Pictured p. 105

SERVES 4 TO 6

WINE PAIRING: Gorman The Devil You Know

This rustic Mediterranean octopus dish is full flavored but approachable. The Devil You Know is a clean-tasting, Cab-forward Bordeaux blend with warmer spice notes to complement the richness of the hazelnuts in the romesco sauce. It's also aggressive enough to balance the char from the savory grilled octopus and the sweeter stems of the broccolini.

OCTOPUS In a stockpot, combine all ingredients except the octopus. Add 2 quarts of water and bring to a boil. Reduce heat to medium-low and simmer for 20 minutes.

Add octopus and gently simmer for 2 hours, until very tender and fully cooked. (To check the doneness, cut off a tentacle from the body and slice a piece. If the texture is rubbery, cook octopus for another 15 minutes and check again.) Transfer octopus to a large bowl and set aside to cool, then remove the tentacles and set aside until use, discarding the rest.

HAZELNUT ROMESCO Preheat oven to 300°F.

Place tomatoes on a baking sheet and roast for 40 minutes, until slightly dehydrated.

In a small saucepan, combine garlic and oil and cook over medium heat for 25 minutes, until tender and slightly caramelized.

In a food processor, grind hazelnuts until very fine. With the motor still running, add the roasted tomatoes, piquillo peppers, caramelized garlic, and garlic-infused oil. Add vinegar and season with salt and pepper. Set aside.

OCTOPUS
- 1 (8- to 10-oz) can crushed tomatoes
- 1 onion, chopped
- 3 cloves garlic, chopped
- 1 orange, unpeeled and roughly chopped
- 1 lemon, unpeeled and roughly chopped
- 2 bay leaves
- 2 Tbsp kosher salt
- 1 tsp black peppercorns
- 1 tsp fennel seeds
- 1 cup white wine
- 1 (4 to 6 lb) fresh whole octopus

HAZELNUT ROMESCO
- 1 cup cherry tomatoes
- ½ cup garlic cloves
- ¾ cup extra-virgin olive oil
- 2 cups hazelnuts, toasted and peeled
- 8 oz canned piquillo peppers, well rinsed
- ⅓ cup sherry vinegar
- Salt and black pepper, to taste

BROCCOLINI
3 bunches broccolini
Extra-virgin olive oil, for drizzling
Salt, to taste

SHERRY GASTRIQUE
¼ cup sherry vinegar
3 Tbsp granulated sugar
Pinch of salt

ASSEMBLY
¼ cup chopped toasted and
    peeled hazelnuts, for garnish

BROCCOLINI Bring a large saucepan of salted water to a boil. Add broccolini and boil for 30 seconds, until tender but not mushy. Drain, then spread out on a plate to cool. Drizzle with oil and season with salt.

SHERRY GASTRIQUE Combine all ingredients in a small saucepan and cook over medium heat for 15 minutes, until syrupy.

ASSEMBLY Preheat grill to high heat.

Add octopus tentacles and broccolini and grill for about 7 minutes, turning occasionally, until the tentacles are warmed through, charred, and slightly caramelized.

Place a heaping spoon of romesco sauce on each plate and smear it across. Artfully arrange the broccolini and tentacles. Sprinkle hazelnuts and drizzle sherry gastrique on top.

DEVILED SALMON "SHANK," Smoked Walla Walla Onions, and Polenta

CHEF: CAROLYNN SPENCE, SHAKER + SPEAR

SERVES 4

WINE PAIRING: Gorman The Devil You Don't Know

Carolynn Spence's deviled salmon "shank" sees a spicy glazed salmon wrapped around rich marrowbone. Plus, most of the components can be prepared ahead of time, which makes it ideal to serve when you're looking for fuss-free entertaining.

The dish demands a bold pairing, and Gorman Winery's Syrah-forward Rhône blend is a rich complement. I recommend listening to late 1970s punk while dancing with these devils.

POLENTA In a large saucepan, combine butter, salt, and 4 cups of water and bring to a boil. Slowly whisk in polenta (or cornmeal), then reduce heat to low. Cook for 35 minutes, stirring constantly, until creamy and cooked through. Set aside and keep warm.

SMOKED WALLA WALLA ONIONS In a bowl, combine onion, oil, and salt and set aside to marinate for 20 minutes.

Preheat a smoker to 240°F. Place wood chips in the smoker. (Alternatively, put chips into a heatproof pan and cover with a piece of aluminum foil. Pierce holes throughout, 2 inches apart, to allow the smoke to waft out.) Add onion rings and smoke for 15 to 20 minutes.

Transfer onion rings to a bowl, cover with plastic wrap, and steam for 10 minutes. Cool to room temperature. Add parsley, capers, a squeeze of lemon, and a touch of oil and mix well.

POLENTA

1 cup (2 sticks) butter
2 tsp kosher salt
½ cup coarse yellow polenta or cornmeal

SMOKED WALLA WALLA ONIONS

2 Walla Walla onions or any other sweet variety, sliced into ½-inch rounds
2 Tbsp olive oil, plus extra for finishing
2 tsp kosher salt
Alderwood, cherry wood, and/or applewood chips
1 cup chopped parsley
3 Tbsp capers (from brine)
1 lemon wedge

SALMON "SHANK"

6 Tbsp prepared horseradish
¼ cup ketchup
¼ cup Dijon mustard
¼ cup maple syrup
¼ cup canned tomatoes, puréed
¼ cup Worcestershire sauce
½ Tbsp Aleppo pepper
1 tsp smoked paprika
½ tsp kosher salt
½ tsp black pepper
4 marrowbones, 2½ inches long
4 skinless salmon steaks, 2 inches
   thick

SALMON "SHANK" In a bowl, combine all ingredients except the bone marrow and salmon. Set aside for at least 30 minutes. (The longer it sits, the more time the spices have to "bloom.")

Preheat oven to 400°F. Line a baking sheet with parchment paper.

Place marrowbones on the prepared baking sheet and roast for 10 minutes. Remove from the oven and set aside to cool to room temperature.

Wrap a salmon steak around each marrowbone to imitate a shank. Tie kitchen twine around each "shank" and secure it with a knot. (You don't want to knot it too tight, just enough to hold the salmon in place.) Roast for 5 minutes. Remove from the oven and brush glaze all over the salmon, avoiding the marrowbone. Roast for another 10 minutes. Cut off twine.

ASSEMBLY Ladle polenta onto each plate. Using a spatula, gently place a salmon shank on top of polenta. Place the Walla Walla onions next to the shank. Accompany dish with a small spoon in each marrow, for scooping.

GUARDIAN CELLARS

+

JERRY RIENER AND JENNIFER SULLIVAN

When discussing the winemaking industry, it's rare to find someone who was inspired by a piece of farm equipment. But when you ask Jerry Riener what it was that sparked his interest in the business, he'll tell you it was a forklift.

As a kid, Jerry spent lots of time visiting relatives on the farms of Kansas. "I drove every piece of John Deere equipment out there, but I'd never driven a forklift." That is until 1997, when he spotted one parked in front of Matthews Winery (page 170), which he happened upon on his way home from work as a Lynn-wood police officer. He immediately volunteered to work at the Woodinville winery, where he would—in addition to driving a forklift—meet an inspiring young winemaker named Mark Ryan McNeilly (page 160), whose winery Jerry helped to open in 1999.

In 2004, Mark repaid the favor by helping Jerry open Guardian. Jerry kept his full-time job as a cop

but made wines in his free time. It's a schedule he keeps to this day, with the help of his wife and business partner, Jennifer Sullivan, whom he met at a crime scene back in 2002. (He was a detective, and she was a crime reporter for the *Seattle Times*.)

"When I started dating Jerry, he told me that if this was going to work out, I would have to learn about wine!" says Jen, who started her compulsory work in the tasting room, securing her love for both wine and her boyfriend.

Guardian wines are bold and friendly. "I love big, rich, ripe wines," says Jerry, "but I still want them to have fresh characteristics

with good acid." A great starting point is the Chalk Line. This blend of Cabernet Sauvignon, Merlot, and Syrah from each of their vine-yards (Columbia Valley, Wahluke Slope, and Red Mountain) is a true expression of Washington wines.

The flavors are very different depending on varietal or blend, but it's the consistent style across all the varieties that makes the wines so popular. Says Jerry, "We want our wines to have structure, depth, and great fruit behind them, but they shouldn't be fruit bombs." These wines can be consumed as soon as they're bottled but will age for fifteen years. He adds, "We're like the Goldilocks of wine-making: we want everything we make to be just right."

SHELLFISH with Saffron Sofrito

CHEF: MATT JANKE, LECOSHO

SOFRITO

1 cup fruity, full-bodied olive oil
1 cup assorted bell peppers, chopped
1 small sweet onion, chopped (½ cup)
2 cloves garlic, thinly sliced
2 generous pinches saffron threads
1 bay leaf
2 Tbsp kosher salt

SHELLFISH

2 Tbsp fruity, full-bodied olive oil, plus extra to serve
3 oz Spanish chorizo or any hard sausage, peeled and diced (about ½ cup)
12 oz clams, cleaned
12 oz mussels, scrubbed, cleaned, and drained well
½ bottle cava or any inexpensive dry sparkling wine
Sofrito (see here)
8 prawns or shrimp, peeled and deveined
1 to 2 Tbsp cold butter, cubed
Chopped herbs, such as parsley, chives, and/or cilantro
Grated zest of 1 lemon
Finishing salt, to taste
Crusty bread, to serve
Good-quality extra-virgin olive oil or butter, to serve

WINE PAIRING: Guardian Angel Sauvignon Blanc

Sofrito—the Spanish term for "lightly fried"—is an essential component to fish stews and paella. The wine's grapefruit notes and acidity are excellent with the richness of the shellfish, while its full-bodied finish stands up to the saffron and peppers in the sauté.

SOFRITO Heat oil in a heavy-bottomed saucepan over medium-high heat, until the surface shimmers. Add the remaining ingredients and stir to incorporate. Simmer for 5 to 7 minutes, then remove from heat and set aside. (The sofrito can be stored in the refrigerator for up to 2 weeks.)

SHELLFISH Heat oil in a heavy-bottomed saucepan or Dutch oven over high heat. Add chorizo and sauté, until the chorizo begins to brown. Add clams and mussels.

Pour in cava and sofrito. Bring to a boil, then reduce the heat and cover. Simmer for 5 to 6 minutes, until clams and mussels have begun to open. Stir in prawns (or shrimp) and cover. Simmer for another 2 to 3 minutes, until prawns turn pink and opaque. Stir in butter and remove from heat. Discard any unopened mussels and clams. Add herbs and lemon zest and season with finishing salt.

Ladle shellfish into bowls and serve with crusty bread and oil (or butter).

COFFEE-BRAISED SHORT
RIBS with Gremolata CHEF: MATT JANKE, LECOSHO

SHORT RIBS

1 cup kosher salt, plus extra
  to taste
1 cup light brown cane sugar
2 Tbsp ground coriander
¼ cup dark roast instant coffee
  granules
5 lbs bone-in beef short ribs,
  with the bone cut lengthwise
2 Tbsp olive oil
1 onion, chopped (½ cup)
1 carrot, chopped (½ cup)
1 stalk celery, chopped
1 rutabaga, chopped (½ cup)
3 cloves garlic, chopped
2 cups dry red wine
1 (6-oz) can tomato paste

GREMOLATA

Bunch of parsley, chopped
2 Tbsp finely chopped shallot
2 Tbsp grated horseradish
Grated zest of 1 lemon
2 tsp flaky sea salt

ASSEMBLY

Buttered noodles or polenta,
  to serve
Finishing salt, for sprinkling

WINE PAIRING: Guardian Chalk Line Red Blend

These tender, slow-braised ribs make for an intensely
flavorful and fragrant entrée. Chef Matt Janke recommends
bone-in beef ribs, but you can also use boneless ribs if you
prefer. A bright and zesty gremolata—consisting of chopped
herbs, shallot, and citrus—is sprinkled over the ribs just
before serving.

Guardian Cellars' robust red blend—with its Cabernet
Sauvignon, Merlot, and Syrah—has enough tannin to stand
alongside beef, and the blackberry and plum notes pair well
with the aromatic rub.

SHORT RIBS In a bowl, combine salt, sugar, coriander, and
instant coffee. Generously coat the ribs with the rub, shake
off any excess seasoning, and put the ribs in a bowl or glass
dish fatty-side down. Cover and refrigerate overnight.

Preheat oven to 375°F. Brush off excess rub from the ribs.

Heat oil in a large Dutch oven over medium-high heat.
Add ribs fatty-side down and sear for 5 to 6 minutes, until
brown. Turn over ribs, then add onion, carrot, celery, rutabaga, and garlic and cook for 5 to 6 minutes, until vegetables
are browned. Stir in wine and tomato paste and bring to a
boil. Cover and place in the oven and cook for 40 minutes.

Reduce heat to 325°F. Braise ribs for 3 hours, until tender
and meat falls from the bone. Gently transfer ribs to a plate
and set aside.

Skim fat from braising liquid, then simmer over medium-
high heat for 10 to 15 minutes, until it's reduced to a thick
sauce. Season with salt to taste.

GREMOLATA In a bowl, combine all ingredients and
set aside.

ASSEMBLY Place buttered noodles (or polenta) on a large
serving platter or individual plates. Ladle sauce over the
noodles. Top with ribs, sprinkle with salt, and garnish with
gremolata.

HARD ROW TO HOE VINEYARDS

+

JUDY AND DON PHELPS

Winemaking is a second career for Judy Phelps, who started out as a biostatistician for a pharmaceutical company. It's a job title that takes several glasses of wine just to comprehend. Just ask Judy—who was making wine in her garage during her tenure in corporate America.

After moving to Washington from the East Coast in 2000, she and her husband, Don, who is a civil engineer, traveled up to British Columbia, Canada, to explore the Okanagan Valley, a region renowned for its wines. "We were impressed with all of the family-run boutique wineries and had a chance to meet and chat with the winemakers and owners," she explains. "We became enamored with the lifestyle, so I asked Don if we should start a winery." The rest, as they say, is history.

The two bought an apple orchard in Lake Chelan, pulled out the apple trees, and planted vines. Judy even went back to school to get her winemaking certificate from UC Davis. In 2005, Hard Row to Hoe opened its doors. "Don loves to be on his tractor more than he loves being at his civil-engineering desk, and I love making wine."

Hard Row is organic, certified sustainable, and salmon safe. "We run the only vineyard in north central Washington that farms this way. We only use organic certified materials on the vineyard."

And if there's a new grape available, Judy wants to experiment with it, which makes it challenging to pinpoint which wines she's making at any given time. Their Cabernet Franc is the flagship, but they've also received accolades for their Tempranillo, Riesling, and Pinot Noir.

Don and Judy are passionate about growing grapes and making wine from the Lake Chelan Valley. As one of the pioneer wineries in the region, they are helping to define the Lake Chelan terroir with their focus on single-varietal, single-vineyard wines. In many ways, growing grapes and making estate wines is still a big science experiment that Don and Judy are more than happy to indulge in by making a variety of different, small-batch wines.

> Shrimp and Leek Chowder | p. 116

SHRIMP AND LEEK
CHOWDER CHEF: BEN DAVISON, CHARTER HOTEL

Pictured p. 115

SERVES 4 TO 6

WINE PAIRING: Hard Row to Hoe Glacial Gravels Vineyard Dry Riesling

This tasty dish pays homage to the bounty of produce in late spring—when leeks are still young and tender, new potatoes are at their best, and fresh shrimp are caught along the Oregon and Washington coast. To make the shellfish stock, ask your fishmonger if they have any shells on hand, or buy head-on shrimp, which are usually available at Asian markets or specialty seafood purveyors.

The sweet, tropical flavors of Hard Row to Hoe's Riesling balances out the intensity of the broth and makes this rich, creamy chowder even more delectable.

SHELLFISH STOCK

1 cup olive oil (divided)
4 cups shellfish shells
3 carrots, chopped
3 stalks celery, chopped
1 yellow onion, chopped
1 leek, chopped
1 head garlic, peeled and chopped
2 Tbsp kosher salt
½ cup tomato paste
½ cup white wine
½ bunch parsley, roughly chopped

SHELLFISH STOCK Heat 1 tablespoon oil in a stockpot over high heat. Add shells and using a wooden spoon or rubber spatula, stir vigorously for 3 to 5 minutes, until fragrant. Add carrots, celery, onion, leek, garlic, and salt. Reduce heat to medium-low, add the remaining oil, and cook for 5 minutes.

Add tomato paste and stir to coat vegetables and shells. Add wine, scraping the caramelized bits off the bottom of the pan. Pour in 2 quarts water, stir in parsley, and simmer for 2 hours over medium-low heat, until fragrant. Strain and set aside. (Makes 2 quarts.)

SHRIMP AND LEEK CHOWDER

5 Tbsp olive oil (divided)
1 small onion, thinly sliced
6 cloves garlic, chopped
3 stalks celery, chopped
2 quarts Shellfish Stock (see here)
1 cup heavy cream
1 cup Riesling
3 Tbsp paprika
3 Tbsp dried oregano
½ cup arborio or sushi rice
3 young leeks, thickly sliced
    (2 cups)
1 cup new potatoes, finely
    chopped
¼ cup (½ stick) butter
½ cup chopped bacon
2 cups chopped raw shrimp meat
¼ cup chopped chives
¼ cup chopped parsley, for
    garnish (optional)
Salt and white pepper, to taste

SHRIMP AND LEEK CHOWDER   Preheat oven to 375°F.

Heat 1 tablespoon oil in a large saucepan over medium heat. Add onion, garlic, and celery. Pour in stock, cream, and wine. Stir in paprika and oregano and cook until it begins to simmer (increase heat if necessary). Add rice and cook for another 20 minutes, until rice is cooked through. Transfer mixture to a blender, in batches, and process until smooth. Set aside.

On a baking sheet, toss leeks in 2 tablespoons oil (or just enough to coat) and roast for 20 minutes, until fully cooked and slightly caramelized.

Meanwhile, heat 2 tablespoons oil in a skillet over high heat. Add potatoes and sear for 3 to 5 minutes on each side, until lightly browned. Transfer potatoes to a baking dish and roast for 20 minutes, until tender.

Combine potatoes and leeks and set aside.

Melt butter in a large saucepan over medium heat. Add bacon and cook for 10 to 12 minutes, until well colored and fat has rendered. Pour in the rice stock, gradually at first to fry slightly in the fat. Stir quickly, then bring to a light simmer. Add leeks, potatoes, shrimp, and herbs. Cook for another minute, then season with salt and white pepper.

Ladle chowder into bowls and garnish with parsley. Serve immediately.

VEAL RIBS with Juniper and Turnips
CHEF: BEN DAVISON, CHARTER HOTEL

SERVES 6

WINE PAIRING: Hard Row to Hoe Burning Desire Cabernet Franc

At the restaurant, the ribs are smoked over applewood, but you can get similar results by braising the veal and finishing it off on a hot grill. The inexpensive ribs, which are part of the breast, can be ordered from a quality butcher. Be sure to start this recipe a day in advance so the veal has enough time to cook and then cool before hitting the grill.

And with the spicy juniper sauce and rich roasted turnips, the dish sings alongside the rich, jammy fruitiness of the Cabernet.

VEAL RIBS Preheat oven to 375°F. Season ribs with salt and pepper.

Heat oil in a large skillet over high heat, until just smoking. Working in batches, sear ribs for 7 to 10 minutes, until well browned on all sides. Transfer to a plate and set aside. Add onion, garlic, leek, and celery and sauté for 5 minutes, scraping the caramelized bits off the bottom of the pan. Add juniper and stir, until fragrant.

Add ribs, pour in stock and wine, and braise for 2 hours, until tender. Strain into a bowl, reserving 3½ cups of the braising liquid. Discard vegetables and set aside the veal ribs to cool.

JUNIPER SAUCE Pour 2 cups of the braising liquid into a saucepan. Add the remaining ingredients except for the butter and cook over medium-high heat for 45 minutes, until thickened and reduced to a quarter of the original amount. Strain, then stir in butter until completely melted. Set aside.

VEAL RIBS
½ veal breast, cut into 6 individual ribs
Salt and black pepper, to taste
1 cup olive oil, plus extra if needed
1 yellow onion, sliced
1 head garlic, peeled
1 leek, chopped
3 stalks celery, chopped
2 Tbsp dried juniper berries
4 cups chicken stock
1 (750-ml) bottle red wine

JUNIPER SAUCE
2 cups veal braising liquid (see here)
2 shallots, finely sliced
¼ cup granulated sugar
1 clove, ground
1½ Tbsp dried juniper berries, ground
½ tsp ground coriander
½ cup sherry or apple cider vinegar
½ cup (1 stick) cold butter, cubed

2 bunches young white turnips,
cut into wedges
1½ cups veal braising liquid (see
here)
¼ cup (½ stick) cold butter,
cubed
¼ cup chopped chives
Salt and black pepper, to taste

Olive oil, for brushing
Salt and black pepper, to taste

TURNIPS Preheat oven to 375°F.

Heat an ovenproof skillet over high heat. Add turnips cut-side down and sear for 5 minutes, until well browned. Roast in the oven for 15 minutes, until tender. Remove from the oven, add braising liquid and butter and roast for another 15 minutes, until turnips are glazed and liquid is reduced. Add chives and season with salt and pepper.

ASSEMBLY Preheat grill to high heat.

Brush oil over ribs, then season with salt and pepper. Place ribs on the grill and sear quickly, charring all sides. (If you happen to be near a spruce or juniper tree, throw some small branches into the fire to add a fresh smoky flavor.)

Transfer ribs to a serving platter and spoon juniper sauce over the top. Serve with turnips.

HAWKINS CELLARS

+

THANE HAWKINS

As a former visual-effects artist for Pixar and Dreamworks, Thane Hawkins contributed to popular films such as *Antz*, *Shrek*, and *Monsters, Inc.*, but always felt a nagging pull toward the great outdoors. "I have never been an office kind of person, and it started to feel out of balance with my interest in the natural world."

While working in the Bay Area and with California wine country in his backyard, Thane developed a passion for Rhône wine varietals, as well as Pinot Noir. He decided to take a six-month sabbatical and beelined to Portland and the Willamette Valley, "and that's where I started getting more involved with wine."

Thane enrolled in wine studies at Chemeketa College in Salem, Oregon, and was eventually hired as the assistant winemaker for Methven Family Vineyards, where he started making some wine under the Hawkins Cellars label in 2007.

In 2011, Thane opened his own tasting room in Dundee, Oregon, followed by a second tasting room on Underwood Mountain in the Columbia Gorge in 2017. "I was already sourcing fruit from Yakima Valley, so it made sense to move the operation a little bit closer to that fruit."

Sitting at an elevation of 1,400 feet, Hawkins' Underwood location is similar in climate to the Alsace region of France. Here, Thane is both growing and sourcing cool-climate grapes such as Chardonnay and Pinot Noir, as well as Pinot Gris and Gewürztraminer, which he uses to make his TruNorth white blend.

Named by *Travel + Leisure* as one of the top wineries in the U.S. for 2017, Hawkins also continues to focus on Rhône-style wines such as their signature Caldera Red, a blend of Mourvèdre, Grenache, Syrah, and Viognier. "When you open it, it evolves from black cherry to black fruit as it softens," explains Thane. "With all my wines, I like seeing that development of the wine as soon as the bottle is opened."

WILD BOAR BOLOGNESE

with Penne COURTESY OF MARX FOODS

⅓ cup dried porcini mushrooms
2 Tbsp extra-virgin olive oil
1 small onion, finely chopped
1 small carrot, finely chopped
1 small stalk celery, finely
    chopped
1½ oz pancetta, finely chopped
1 bay leaf
¾ tsp kosher salt (divided)
Black pepper
2 small cloves garlic, finely
    chopped
½ Tbsp finely chopped rosemary
1 lb ground wild boar
½ cup dry white wine
½ (20-oz) can fire-roasted whole
    tomatoes with juices
1 cup low- or no-sodium pork or
    chicken stock
½ tsp chili flakes
½ cup heavy cream
1 lb high-quality dried penne
    (preferably Filotea's Pennette
    della Domenica)
¼ cup grated Parmesan, plus
    extra for garnish

WINE PAIRING: Hawkins Cellars Caldera Red

Lean and high in protein, wild boar makes a flavorful alternative to beef and pork. In this classic Italian recipe, a rich ragù makes the ideal vehicle for flavorful boar. This recipe makes twice as much sauce as required in the recipe, so you can either double the pasta to feed a crowd or freeze the rest.

Place porcini in a bowl, cover with boiling water, and set aside for 20 minutes, until mushrooms are tender. Drain mushrooms and reserve liquid.

Heat oil in a large saucepan over medium-high heat. Add onion, carrot, celery, pancetta, bay leaf, ½ teaspoon salt, and pepper. Cook for 7 to 10 minutes, until vegetables are browned and fat is rendered. Finely chop porcini and add to pan. Stir in garlic and rosemary.

Add wild boar and cook for another 10 minutes, until browned. Break up chunks. Pour in wine. Add reserved porcini liquid.

Add tomatoes, stock, chili flakes, and remaining ¼ teaspoon salt.

Bring the liquid to a boil, then reduce the heat to a simmer. Cover and simmer for at least 1 hour. Uncover, increase heat to medium and simmer, stirring often until sauce has thickened to a desired consistency. Remove bay leaf and pour in cream. Keep warm.

Bring a large saucepan of salted water to a boil and cook pasta according to package instructions, until it's very al dente. Drain.

Stir Parmesan into the sauce. Add pasta and heat through. Serve on a large serving platter or in individual bowls and garnish with Parmesan.

MOREL AND LEEK DUTCH BABY
COURTESY OF MARX FOODS

TOMATO JAM
2 Tbsp olive oil
½ onion, finely chopped
Sprig of rosemary
3 Tbsp granulated sugar (divided)
1 (28-oz) can fire-roasted whole tomatoes, cut up with kitchen shears
½ cup red wine vinegar
1 tsp grated orange zest
1 clove garlic, finely chopped
2 Tbsp finely chopped basil leaves
Salt and black pepper, to taste

DUTCH BABY
½ oz dried morels
1½ cups all-purpose flour
1½ cups whole milk
1 tsp kosher salt, plus extra to taste
6 eggs
3 Tbsp butter (divided)
1 leek, white portion only, finely sliced
1 tsp chopped thyme
Grated Parmesan

WINE PAIRING: Hawkins Cellars Chardonnay

Dutch babies are a cross between pancakes and popovers: fluffy, eggy, and absolutely delicious. While they're traditionally a sweet breakfast food, there's no reason they can't be savory instead.

TOMATO JAM Heat oil in a nonreactive sauté pan over medium-high heat. Add onion and rosemary. Sprinkle 1½ tablespoons sugar over onion, reduce heat to medium-low, and sauté for 10 to 15 minutes, until well caramelized.

Add tomatoes (with their juice), vinegar, remaining 1½ tablespoons sugar, orange zest, and garlic. Increase heat to medium-high and cook for 15 minutes, until it has a jam-like consistency. Stir in basil, then season with salt and pepper.

DUTCH BABY Place morels in a bowl and cover with boiling water. Set aside for at least 20 minutes, until the mushrooms are tender. Strain the mushrooms, reserving the liquid, and slice them into rings.

Preheat oven to 400°F. Place a large cast-iron skillet in the oven.

In a bowl, whisk together flour, milk, salt, and eggs. (It's okay if it's lumpy.) Strain batter.

Melt 2 tablespoons butter in another skillet over medium heat. Add leek and a pinch of salt. Sauté for 8 to 10 minutes, until the leek is softened and browned.

Add morels, thyme, and 1 cup of reserved morel liquid. Simmer for 5 to 7 minutes, until liquid has evaporated.

Heat the remaining tablespoon of butter in the preheated cast-iron skillet. Add the morel mixture, stir, and pour in batter. Bake for 20 to 25 minutes, until the Dutch baby is well puffed. (Do not open the door before the 20-minute mark or it will deflate!)

Serve immediately, topped with Parmesan and tomato jam on the side.

HEDGES FAMILY ESTATE

+

SARAH HEDGES GOEDHART

It's been said that the best way to learn is to go beyond limits and set your own rules, and this is certainly the case for Hedges Family Estate, whose rise to success has been nothing short of impressive.

The Hedges winery was born in the late 1980s when Tom and Anne-Marie Hedges purchased a plot of land in the Columbia Valley and planted Bordeaux grapes. In 1995, they broke ground on their château-style tasting room—a gorgeous landscaped oasis in the Columbia Valley that, in 2001, became the celebrated Red Mountain appellation.

Winemaker Sarah Hedges Goedhart grew up in the family wine business, but she officially joined the team as an assistant winemaker in 2005. Ten years later, she would become head winemaker, managing and producing wines from four estate vineyards on Red Mountain totaling 130 acres, which are now all farmed using organic and biodynamic practices (Hedges is one of only three certified biodynamic farms in the state and has the only certified biodynamic wine in the state). She is passionate about Syrah and, along with the Hedges wines, produces her own Red Mountain Syrah under the label Goedhart Family.

Sarah has helped to raise the profile of the family business, earning them various awards and distinctions. Her first vintage, the 2015 Hedges Family Estate CMS (Cabernet Sauvignon, Merlot, Syrah), earned her one of *Sunset* magazine's Top Wines of 2018. Her 2014 Descendants Liégeois Dupont (DLD) Syrah won myriad accolades, including Wine of the Year and a Double Gold from the Sommeliers Choice Awards 2019.

Sarah considers herself more of a "fermentation guidance counselor" than winemaker because nothing is used to manipulate the end product. "The biggest decision I make is when to pick the grapes, which defines the wine, and from there, I just guide it along."

> *Côte de Boeuf* | p. 126

CÔTE DE BOEUF

CHEF: BRENDAN MCGILL, HITCHCOCK

Pictured p. 125

SERVES 2 TO 4

WINE PAIRING: Hedges Family Estate La Haute Cuvée Biodynamic Cabernet Sauvignon

In French cuisine, a rib steak with the bone attached is called côte de boeuf. At Hitchcock, chef Brendan McGill prefers a single-rib width as it makes the perfect amount for a handsome dinner for two. Buy good-quality grass-fed meat: dry-aged beef will yield a more tender and flavorful result, so look for something that's twenty-one days or older. You can also ask your butcher for the cut nearest the shoulder, which will have the most intramuscular marbling and roundest shape.

CÔTE DE BOEUF Unwrap steak and set it on a small roasting rack. Grab 1 tablespoon sea salt (that's a three-finger pinch), and from a 12-inch height above the steak (this ensures an even spread of the salt), sprinkle the salt generously all over the steak until well seasoned. Really lay it on thick. Most of the salt will fall off anyway. Set aside on the counter to rest for an hour.

Fill your chimney starter halfway with lump (hardwood) charcoal (not briquettes), and place a couple sheets of crumpled newspaper under the chimney. Light the paper and allow to burn for 5 minutes, until coals are bright red. Pour the hot coals into the grill and continue to heat until it's screaming hot.

Using a wire brush, clean the surface of the grill. Lay steak over the red-hot coals, taking care as it will flame up. When the flames engulf the steak, cover with the top and slightly crack open the air vents on the top and bottom. (This keeps the flames down while the coals apply strong direct heat and impart a thick layer of smoke.)

CÔTE DE BOEUF

1 bone-in rib-eye steak
  (a full rib-width is best)
1 Tbsp sea salt
6 Tbsp high-quality demi-glace
  (see Note)
1 Tbsp butter, room
  temperature

NOTE: Demi-glace (veal glaze) is a gourmet item that can be found at fine food stores or via Amazon. Alternatively, use a premium beef base (located in the soup and stock aisle of supermarkets) and thicken with a little cornstarch.

ASSEMBLY
Roasted root vegetables or lightly
    dressed salad greens, to serve
Smoked salt or other finishing
    salt, to taste

Cook for 5 minutes. Rotate steak 45 degrees and cook for another 5 minutes. Turn over and repeat. Cook until the steak reaches an internal temperature of 120°F for medium-rare. If the coals are dying, open the air vents a little more, but keep an eye on the flame to make sure you're not incinerating the steak. (You do not want to eat rib eye rare or blue-rare. The fat isn't warm enough to soften up and match the texture of the tender meat.)

Transfer steak to a roasting rack and cover loosely with aluminum foil. Set aside for 20 to 30 minutes. (You don't want to wrap it and steam it but rather just keep the chill off of it.)

In a small saucepan, heat up demi-glace over medium heat and stir in butter. Remove from heat.

ASSEMBLY Transfer steak to a wooden cutting board. Using a sharp knife, slice the bone off steak. Working perpendicular to the bone, slice steak into thin strips, keeping them arranged as they were when intact. Slide knife under the strips and transfer to a serving platter. Lay bone next to the sliced beef, sort of reassembled in its natural form. Sprinkle with salt, then pour demi-glace on top. Serve with root vegetables or a side salad.

PÂTÉ DE CAMPAGNE

CHEF: BRENDAN MCGILL, HITCHCOCK

MAKES 2 TERRINES

WINE PAIRING: Hedges Family Estate Red Mountain Blend

This signature pâté at Hitchcock is wrapped in a house-smoked bacon and served either on a plate or in a baguette. A wine needs to be equally bold to stand up to the confident flavors of the pâté, and Hedges Family Estate's flagship blend does just that with its lingering fruity notes, which give way to smoke and leather.

You'll want to invest in a meat grinder, even an inexpensive manual one, to achieve the silky texture of the pâté.

PÂTÉ DE CAMPAGNE Chop the pork shoulder, liver, and 8 ounces of the fatback into 1-inch cubes. Transfer to a large bowl, and combine with shallot, garlic, salt, Insta Cure #1, pepper, and quatre épices.

In a separate bowl, combine cream, baguette, brandy, and eggs (this is called *panade*) and set aside for 1 hour, until bread is soggy. Add this to the bowl of pork. Run the mixture through a meat grinder with a medium-large grinder plate. Repeat a second time through a smaller grinder plate for a smoother texture. Finely chop the remaining 6 ounces of fatback. Add this and the pistachios to the bowl and mix evenly.

Preheat oven to 325°F.

PÂTÉ DE CAMPAGNE

3 lbs pork shoulder
1 lb pork liver
14 oz pork fatback, divided
2 large shallots, finely chopped
6 cloves garlic, chopped
2½ Tbsp kosher salt
1 tsp Insta Cure #1
1 tsp black pepper
¼ tsp quatre épices (see Note)
½ cup heavy cream
3 oz baguette, cut into ½-inch cubes
1 fl oz brandy
2 eggs
½ cup shelled and blanched pistachios
Butter or cooking spray
1 lb thinly sliced bacon

Dijon mustard
Fruit preserves
Frisée
Crusty baguette

NOTE: Quatre épices is literally "four spices"—usually white pepper, nutmeg, ginger, and cloves. It's used to season pâtés, sausages, and terrines, as well as soups and stews. Find it online or at specialty grocers.

Rub terrine molds with a thin layer of butter (or cooking spray). Cut a sheet of thick plastic wrap large enough to fit the terrine with a 2-inch overhang on either side. Line the mold. Arrange bacon crosswise, slightly overlapping and hanging off both sides. Gently press the wrap into the corners of the mold, then fill with pâté and spread evenly. Pat down to remove air bubbles, then give the mold a couple firm bangs on the table to remove more of those bubbles. Fold the bacon over the mixture, then fold the plastic wrap neatly on top. Cover with a terrine lid or aluminum foil.

Place the terrine in a deep roasting pan and fill the pan halfway with boiling water.

Cook in the oven for 1 hour, until the internal temperature reaches 145°F. (Using a quick-read thermometer, pierce the top of the plastic mold.)

Remove mold from the water bath. Place something flat and heavy on top (which will help make it firm). Refrigerate overnight.

ASSEMBLY Place mold in a shallow bath of warm water to melt the fat between the mold and the plastic wrap. Turn out onto a cutting board, then slice and enjoy with mustard, fruit preserves, frisée, and baguette!

J. BOOKWALTER WINERY

+

CALEB FOSTER

Ten generations of Bookwalters have gotten their hands dirty in the agriculture business, but it was Jerry Bookwalter who put the family stamp on Washington wine when he planted three iconic vineyards—Sagemoor, Bacchus, and Dionysus—in 1976. And in 1982, J. Bookwalter Winery was born.

Now led by his son John, Bookwalter has grown into a fine winery renowned for high-quality Bordeaux blends led by master winemaker Caleb Foster, who has been in the industry for nearly two decades.

Caleb took a break from college in 1991, and then serendipitously found himself at the door of the iconic Woodward Canyon, looking for a job. "The experience was the opposite of school: there was no paperwork, and it was all hand labor," he explains. "I could prepare products that may not have even existed that morning."

Owner Rick Small, a pioneer in the Washington wine industry, mentored Caleb for eight years, eventually hiring him as the assistant winemaker. In 1998, Caleb moved on to other ventures, landing at J. Bookwalter in 2000, where he made his very first brand of wine called Buty with Nina Buty, who continues to run the winery today. After twelve years, Caleb left to become consulting winemaker for Double Canyon, only to return to J. Bookwalter in 2014 as head winemaker.

"John and I agree on rich, intense, aromatic, and ageable wines. We're not about big tannin monsters; we want our wines to be suave, and we focus on beautiful creaminess."

The winery's flagship tasting room in Richland was named by *Food & Wine* as one of the twenty-three wineries to visit in Washington and Oregon in 2018, thanks in part to its award-winning restaurant Fiction, which the magazine hailed as one of the best winery restaurants in America in 2017.

While John purchased the winery from his parents in 2008, Jerry still manages the vineyards in the Columbia Valley, including Conner-Lee Vineyard, which continues to be a major source of grapes for J. Bookwalter.

> *Chioggia Beets and Burrata* | *p. 132*

CHIOGGIA BEETS AND BURRATA CHEF: DAN MALLAHAN, RIDER

Pictured p. 131

SERVES 4 TO 6

WINE PAIRING: J. Bookwalter Chapter 8 Cabernet Sauvignon

Fresh seasonal ingredients require very little intervention, and this recipe is a harmonious marriage of beets, burrata, and truffles. The beets are salt-baked, a technique used to season the beets and steam them in their own juice, to create a richer flavor and an intense color.

J. Bookwalter's fruit-forward and floral wine Chapter 8 has juicy marionberry and pomegranate notes that work well with this complex salad. Take notice of how the spiced pecans, salty beet purée, and creamy burrata bring out the richness and versatility of the wine.

SPICED PECANS Preheat oven 325°F. Line a baking sheet with parchment paper.

In a large bowl, combine all ingredients until nuts are evenly coated. Place nuts on the prepared baking sheet and bake for 8 to 10 minutes, until golden brown. Set aside for 1 hour to fully cool. The pecans can be stored in an airtight container until needed.

SALT DOUGH–ROASTED BEET PURÉE Preheat oven to 400°F.

Combine flour, salt, and egg whites in large mixing bowl and mix with your hands. Add 1 cup of water and mix until a mass of dough forms. Add a little more water, if needed.

Transfer dough on a lightly dusted counter. Using the palm of your hands, knead for 5 minutes, until smooth and slightly dry but not crumbly.

Carefully encase each beet in dough about ½ inch thick. Place on a wire rack and bake for 2 to 3 hours, until dough is firm, browned, and begins to crack. Set aside to cool.

Crack the dough open and remove beets. (Most of the skin will remain in the dough. Using a dish towel, rub off any remaining skin.) Chop into bite-sized pieces and transfer to a blender. Add oil and purée for 2 minutes, until thick and smooth. (If necessary, add more oil.)

SPICED PECANS

2 cups pecans, quartered
2 Tbsp brown sugar
1 Tbsp kosher salt
1 Tbsp black pepper
1 tsp ground cinnamon
1 tsp Aleppo pepper
½ tsp Szechuan peppercorns, ground
2 Tbsp melted butter

SALT DOUGH–ROASTED BEET PURÉE

6 cups high-gluten all-purpose flour (preferably Shepherd's Grain), plus extra for dusting
2 cups kosher salt
2 egg whites
4 large red beets, unpeeled, stemmed, and trimmed
¼ cup olive oil, plus extra if needed

2 large bunches golf-ball-sized Chioggia beets, unpeeled and stemmed

1 cup olive oil

2 Tbsp kosher salt, plus extra to taste

6 cloves garlic

4 bay leaves

Large sprig of rosemary

4 sprigs thyme

2 sprigs sage

2 Tbsp black peppercorns

1 Tbsp extra-virgin olive oil, plus extra for finishing

1 tsp sherry vinegar (preferably Pedro Ximénez)

2 Tbsp finely chopped chives

Black pepper, to taste

ASSEMBLY

½ lb high-quality burrata

Thinly shaven local Oregon black winter truffles, for garnish (optional)

Spicy arugula, for garnish (optional)

Shaved radish, for garnish (optional)

Finishing salt and black pepper, for sprinkling

Good-quality extra-virgin olive oil, for finishing

Pour purée into a shallow baking pan and set aside to cool. Place a piece of plastic wrap on top to prevent discoloration and a skin from forming. Refrigerate for 2 hours, until fully cooled.

ROASTED CHIOGGIA BEETS Preheat oven to 375°F.

In a bowl, combine beets, 1 cup oil, and salt and toss. Transfer to a deep baking dish, then add garlic, herbs, peppercorns, and 4 cups water. (Water level should cover half of the beets. Add more water if necessary.) Cover with aluminum foil and cook for 2 to 3 hours, until tender to the core. Remove from the oven and set aside for 20 minutes to cool slightly.

Using a dish towel, rub off any skin, keeping roots intact as much as possible. Refrigerate beets for 2 hours. Cut to desired sizes, split in half, or keep whole.

In a bowl, combine beets, 1 tablespoon extra-virgin olive oil, vinegar, chives, and salt and pepper.

ASSEMBLY Smear beet purée on one side of a serving platter. Arrange beets and burrata on the plate, spacing them apart so that the purée is visible. Add a couple spoons of pecans, as well as shaved truffles, spicy arugula, and shaved radish, if using. Then finish with salt and pepper, and lots of oil.

NETTLE GNOCCHI

with Wild Morels and Bee-Pollen
Vinaigrette CHEF: DAN MALLAHAN, RIDER

SERVES 4 TO 6

WINE PAIRING: J. Bookwalter Protagonist

Wonderfully aromatic and earthy morels are paired with delicate, Parisian-style nettle gnocchi. Stinging nettle is a wild, nutrient-rich native green with a superb nutty flavor. (Use garden gloves when washing nettles, and boil the leaves to neutralize the sting.) Sure, this dish requires some advance preparation, but it's well worth the effort.

With notes of blackberry and flowering currant and a peppery finish, J. Bookwalter's Protagonist is a perfect partner to pair with the intricate flavors of this dish.

MOREL MUSHROOMS Place mushrooms in a bowl of water and carefully agitate. Drain and repeat until the water is clean without any trace of grit. Place mushrooms on a paper-towel-lined baking sheet and set aside to dry. Refrigerate overnight.

Heat oil in a large skillet over high heat. Add mushrooms, garlic, and thyme (remove stems once leaves fall off), then season with salt and pepper. Sauté for 2 minutes. Add butter and cook 2 minutes. Stir in 2 tablespoons water and cook for another minute. Discard thyme stems and set aside.

NETTLE GNOCCHI Bring a large saucepan of salted water to a boil. Add nettles (or kale) and cook for 1 to 2 minutes, until wilted. Transfer nettles to a bowl of ice water.

In a blender, combine nettles, chives, milk, and 4 cups water and blend on high speed until thin and smooth. (If necessary, add more water.)

Measure out 4 cups of purée and pour into a large saucepan, then add butter, salt and pepper, and nutmeg and bring to a simmer over medium heat. Whisk in flour, a little at a time, until all the flour is incorporated and mixture has thickened. Reduce heat to medium-low.

Using a spatula, mix for 5 minutes, until mixture begins to pull away from the sides and has thickened. Remove from heat. Stir in an egg and mix well. Repeat until all eggs are incorporated and dough is smooth and silky.

MOREL MUSHROOMS
1 lb morel mushrooms
¼ cup blended oil (or combine
    2 Tbsp canola oil and 2 Tbsp
    olive oil)
4 cloves garlic, crushed
Bunch of thyme
Salt and black pepper, to taste
¼ cup (½ stick) butter

NETTLE GNOCCHI
½ lb nettles or kale, washed,
    stems removed, and chopped
Large bunch of chives
4 cups fat-free milk
3 Tbsp butter
Salt and black pepper, to taste
½ tsp ground nutmeg
4 cups high-gluten all-purpose
    flour, sifted
3 eggs
1 cup grated Parmesan
Olive oil, for drizzling

¾ cup carrot juice
¼ cup turmeric juice (see Note)
2½ Tbsp bee pollen (see Note)
1 Tbsp honey
Juice of ½ lemon
½ tsp kosher salt

TOASTED WALNUT AILLADE
2 cups walnuts, whole
½ cup grated Parmesan
½ Tbsp kosher salt
½ Tbsp black pepper
Grated zest of 1½ lemons
1 cup extra-virgin olive oil

ASSEMBLY
2 Tbsp extra-virgin olive oil
Salt
1 Tbsp butter
Fresh greens, such as arugula,
    Ruby Streaks mustard greens,
    wild garlic flowers, or miner's
    lettuce, or fried nettle leaves

NOTE: Turmeric juice and bee pollen can be found at local farmers' markets or specialty health or organic grocery stores.

Add Parmesan and cook for 4 to 6 minutes over low heat, until well mixed and dough begins to pull off the sides. Divide the dough into thirds and cover each portion tightly in plastic wrap. Set aside for 5 minutes to rest. Keep warm.

Line a baking sheet with parchment and drizzle with oil. Bring a large saucepan of water to a boil, then reduce the heat to a simmer. Transfer a piece of dough into a piping bag with a round ½-inch tip (or cut a ½-inch-diameter opening in the tip). Twist the end of the bag and gently squeeze. Set the piping bag over the pan and using a paring knife, cut off ½-inch segments of dough into the water. Cook for 5 seconds, until the gnocchi rise to the surface.

Using a slotted spoon, transfer gnocchi to the prepared baking sheet and set aside to cool. Drizzle more oil on top and mix gently. Repeat with remaining gnocchi.

Refrigerate for 2 hours, uncovered. (Gnocchi can be kept in an airtight container for up to 4 days.)

BEE-POLLEN VINAIGRETTE Combine all ingredients in a blender and blend on high speed until smooth. Strain through a fine-mesh strainer and set aside.

TOASTED WALNUT AILLADE Preheat oven to 325°F.

Place walnuts in a single layer on a baking sheet and toast for 8 to 12 minutes, until golden brown. Set aside to cool.

Transfer to a food processor and pulse until roughly chopped. In a large bowl, combine walnuts and remaining ingredients and mix well. Set aside.

ASSEMBLY Heat oil in a heavy-bottomed skillet over medium-high heat until it shimmers. Add gnocchi, season with salt, and cook for 1 to 1½ minutes on one side, until browned. Turn over and cook for another 30 seconds until warmed through, then add butter and gently shake the pan to release the gnocchi and coat them evenly in butter. Add morels and cook for another minute until warmed through.

Using a slotted spoon, transfer mixture onto a serving platter. Drizzle with walnut aillade and bee-pollen vinaigrette. (Leftover sauce can be kept refrigerated for up to 5 days.) Finish with fresh greens (or fried nettle leaves).

KIONA VINEYARDS AND WINERY

+

J.J. WILLIAMS

In the late 1960s, John Williams and fellow nuclear engineer Jim Holmes were conducting field trials at WSU to determine the viability of growing wine grapes in Washington. The university needed people who not only understood farming practices but were also scientifically minded to run what were essentially laboratory vineyards. John and Jim fit the bill and saw an opportunity.

In 1972, John and Jim purchased about eighty-five acres of land on Red Mountain, using ten acres to plant the region's first vineyard in 1975. At a time when conventional wisdom dictated that only Riesling and Chardonnay could be grown successfully in Washington, John and Jim dedicated just as much land to Cabernet. They knew the grapes would grow well, having seen it firsthand through their research at WSU. "That's really where they cut their teeth on viticulture in Washington," says

J.J. Williams, who is the director of operations as well as John's grandson. A year after the first block of grapes was planted, they added other varieties including Merlot, Chenin Blanc, and Lemberger.

And that was the birth of the Kiona Estate vineyard. Today, the Williams family grows Red Mountain grapes for more than sixty other Washington wineries. More than half of their 270 acres of planted vineyards is Cabernet, and all of their wines are food friendly. "Our wine is great to drink on its own, but it has the stuffing to match with food," explains J.J., who has been gravitating more

toward the Kiona Merlot and Sangiovese lately. "They have that combination of drinkability, structure, and balance to be your one-bottle-quiver for the evening."

Eventually, the Williams family purchased Holmes's share of the business, but they still remain good friends today—it's a relationship forever rooted by the cocreation of something truly amazing.

BOAR RIBS

½ cup loosely packed brown sugar
½ cup kosher salt
2 Tbsp black pepper
4 lbs wild boar or pork ribs
2 to 3 quarts chicken stock
2 cups Mexican Coca-Cola or regular Coca-Cola

BLACKBERRY-MUSTARD BBQ SAUCE

3 Tbsp butter
1 yellow onion, thinly sliced
4 cloves garlic, chopped
2 Tbsp loosely packed brown sugar
½ Tbsp kosher salt
½ Tbsp smoked paprika
½ tsp ground cinnamon
½ tsp chili powder
1½ Tbsp honey
1 Tbsp molasses
2 cups blackberries
¼ cup huckleberries
½ cup Dijon mustard
½ cup spicy brown mustard (preferably Gulden's)
½ cup apple cider vinegar
¼ cup French's mustard

ASSEMBLY

Scallions, sliced, for garnish
Chili oil, to serve
Cornbread muffins, to serve

BOAR RIBS with Blackberry-Mustard BBQ Sauce CHEF: MITCH MAYERS, SAWYER

WINE PAIRING: Kiona Red Mountain Estate Reserve

Summer barbecue is a treasured pastime in this great state, and Mitch Mayers loves to cook up ribs. Boar is a wonderful change of pace, but classic pork ribs can also be substituted. Served alongside a creamy coleslaw, this is the type of dish you'll want to eat year-round. (Go ahead; I won't judge.)

Kiona's Red Mountain Estate Reserve—with its complex herbaceous quality and firm tannins—highlights the rich smokiness of the ribs. The ripe, dark fruit of the wine is well complemented by the BBQ sauce.

BOAR RIBS In a small bowl, combine brown sugar, salt, and pepper. Rub mixture on both sides of the ribs and place them in a roasting pan. Refrigerate, covered, for 6 to 24 hours.

Bring ribs to room temperature, about 45 minutes.

Preheat oven to 325°F.

Pour stock and cola over ribs and cover dish in parchment and aluminum foil. Cook for 4 hours, until ribs are tender and meat falls off the bone. Uncover ribs and set aside to cool in the liquid for 1 hour.

BLACKBERRY-MUSTARD BBQ SAUCE Melt butter in a large saucepan over medium-low heat. Add onion and garlic and cook for 20 minutes, stirring occasionally. Add brown sugar, salt, paprika, cinnamon, chili powder, honey, and molasses and cook for another 10 minutes, stirring frequently.

Add remaining ingredients and bring to a simmer. Reduce heat to low, and cook for 1 hour. Stir occasionally. Using a hand blender, purée sauce until nearly smooth.

ASSEMBLY Preheat grill to high heat (450°F).

Place ribs on the grill and brush BBQ sauce over both sides. Cook for 2 to 4 minutes on each side, basting each side twice, until hot and the sauce is caramelized. (Alternatively, preheat the broiler. Brush ribs with BBQ sauce and broil on the middle rack for 5 to 6 minutes, until the sauce caramelizes and deepens in color.)

Transfer ribs to a serving platter, garnish with scallions, and serve with chili oil and cornbread muffins.

SPOT PRAWN AND BEEF TENDERLOIN UDON NOODLES

CHEF: MITCH MAYERS, SAWYER

WINE PAIRING: Kiona Red Mountain Lemberger

What's not to love about a bowl of thick noodles in a nourishing and flavorful broth? This signature dish at Sawyer is generally made with house pastrami, but it's been replaced here with tenderloin, which pairs better with Kiona's Lemberger.

The subtle notes of citrus zest in the wine complement the earthiness of sesame and mushroom. The wine has a medium body and enough structure to stand up to the tenderloin, without overpowering the more delicate nature of the prawns.

UDON SAUCE Combine all ingredients in a bowl and whisk until sugar is dissolved.

SPOT PRAWN AND BEEF TENDERLOIN UDON NOODLES
Cut beef tenderloin into thin strips against the grain.

Heat butter in a large skillet over high heat. Add gai lan (or bok choy), bell pepper, carrot, shallot, and mushrooms and sauté for 2 to 3 minutes, until tender. Transfer to bowl.

In the same pan, heat oil over high heat. Add beef and prawns and cook for 2 minutes, stirring to heat through. Add noodles, udon sauce, and the mixed vegetables. Add a squeeze of lime juice and season with salt.

Transfer noodles to a serving platter and garnish with cilantro, if using.

UDON SAUCE
¼ cup granulated sugar
½ tsp paprika
Pinch of cayenne pepper
½ cup soy sauce
½ cup rice vinegar
2 Tbsp sesame oil
1 Tbsp hoisin sauce
½ Tbsp Sriracha

SPOT PRAWN AND BEEF TENDERLOIN UDON NOODLES
½ lb beef tenderloin
1 Tbsp butter
3 gai lan or bok choy, halved lengthwise
1 red bell pepper, deseeded, deveined, and cut into ¼-inch strips
1 carrot, sliced into ¼-inch rounds
1 small shallot, thinly sliced into rings
2 cups maitake or button mushrooms, quartered
1 Tbsp canola oil
1 lb fresh spot prawns, heads removed, peeled and deveined
1 lb udon noodles
½ cup Udon Sauce (see here)
1 lime
Salt, to taste
Sprigs of cilantro, for garnish (optional)

LAUREN ASHTON CELLARS

+

KIT SINGH

Growing up in the Caribbean, Kit Singh wasn't often exposed to great wines. After he moved to Seattle, he fell in with a group of self-taught oenophiles who would take road trips to California wine country. "I was enamored by the beautiful vineyards, which were completely different from the tropical landscape I grew up with."

Despite his exposure to new wines and wine clubs, and while his interest continued to simmer, Kit remained committed to his schoolwork at UW's dental school.

Upon graduation, Kit opened a dental practice in Redmond, but his passion for wine never waned. As he witnessed the Washington wine scene blossom, he returned to school to study enology and viticulture and received a well-rounded education from UC Davis, WSU, and South Seattle College. After volunteering at DeLille Cellars, he launched Lauren Ashton

Cellars in 2009—a winery named after his daughter, Lauren, and son, Ashton.

His 2009 Cuvée Arlette is an elegant example of a Bordeaux-style wine, a blend of Merlot, Cabernet Franc, and Cabernet Sauvignon with a touch of Petit Verdot and Malbec. *Wine Enthusiast* described the limited selection as tight, dark, dense, and perfectly proportioned with the power and tannin to age for decades. His 2017 Riesling was named a Top 100 Wine by *Washington Wine Blog*, and the 2017 Chardonnay and 2018 Rosé both won gold medals at the 2019 Sunset International Wine Competition.

Kit very much identifies as both a dentist and a winemaker, one complementing the other. For a guy who looks at intricately grooved teeth all day, the winemaking offers a welcome respite from the vigor of a dental practice. "Dentistry requires a certain intensity to practice, but the winery has a much more social aspect to it. Although I'm very busy, I get to enjoy both sides," he shares. "I pay close attention to the wine, the grapes, and the vineyard, and what comes into the winery. As you can see from my professions, I enjoy studying the finer details in life."

> *Grilled Salmon with Syrah BBQ Sauce and Corn Risotto* | *p. 142*

GRILLED SALMON with
Syrah BBQ Sauce and Corn Risotto

CHEF: RYAN DONALDSON, GATHER KITCHEN & BAR

Pictured p. 141

SERVES 4

WINE PAIRING: Lauren Ashton Reserve Syrah

The secret to this risotto is a homemade, full-flavored corn stock, but chicken stock can be used in a pinch. Chef Ryan Donaldson also recommends carnaroli rice for a satisfyingly creamy risotto.

We are often taught to pair white wine with fish, but a Washington Syrah pairs nicely with king salmon, especially when grilled. The acidity in the wine cuts the fat of the fish, and the bold, smoky flavors complement one another.

SYRAH BBQ SAUCE Heat oil in a saucepan over medium heat. Add onion and garlic and sauté for 4 minutes, until soft and translucent. Add the remaining ingredients and simmer for 15 to 20 minutes, until the sauce is thick enough to coat the back of a spoon. Set aside.

CORN STOCK Preheat your grill to high heat. Roast corn in the husk for 20 minutes, turning occasionally, until cooked through. Set aside to cool.

Shave the corn kernels from the cob and reserve for the risotto. Cut the cobs in half and place in a large saucepan and add the remaining ingredients. Add enough water to cover the cobs by 2 inches and simmer for 30 minutes. Strain, return to pan, and simmer until needed. (Keeping stock warm makes for a creamier risotto.)

SYRAH BBQ SAUCE

2 Tbsp olive oil
1 yellow onion, finely chopped
2 cloves garlic, finely chopped
1 (8-oz) jar blueberry preserves
1 cup Syrah
1 cup chicken stock
½ cup balsamic vinegar
½ cup red wine vinegar
2 Tbsp molasses
1 Tbsp chili powder
1 Tbsp ground cumin
1 Tbsp ground coriander
1 Tbsp instant coffee granules
2 tsp kosher salt
2 tsp black pepper

CORN STOCK

3 ears of corn, in husks
1 onion, chopped
2 bay leaves
1 Tbsp kosher salt
1 Tbsp black pepper

SWEET CORN RISOTTO

4 oz porcini mushrooms, sliced in half (optional)
2 Tbsp olive oil (divided)
Salt and black pepper, to taste
1 Tbsp canola oil
1 large shallot, finely chopped
3 cloves garlic, finely chopped
1 cup carnaroli rice
4 sprigs thyme, leaves only, chopped
¾ cup white wine
2 cups Corn Stock (see here) or chicken stock, plus extra if needed
2 cups reserved corn kernels
¼ cup smoked Jack cheese (preferably Mt. Townsend Creamery's Campfire)

GRILLED SALMON

Olive oil, for brushing
4 (6-oz) skinless salmon fillets or steaks (preferably king salmon)
Salt and black pepper, to taste
Syrah BBQ Sauce (see here)

ASSEMBLY

Syrah BBQ Sauce (see here)
Chopped herbs, such as chervil, parsley, marjoram, or charred rosemary, for garnish

SWEET CORN RISOTTO Preheat grill to high heat.

Lightly brush porcini, if using, with 1 tablespoon olive oil and sprinkle with a pinch of salt and pepper. Add porcini to the grill and grill for 2 minutes on each side. Transfer to a plate and set aside.

Heat the remaining 1 tablespoon olive oil and canola oil in a large saucepan over medium heat. Add shallot, garlic, and rice and toast lightly, stirring constantly, until rice is nutty and fragrant. (Do not color.) Stir in thyme.

Pour in wine and simmer for 3 to 5 minutes, stirring constantly, until the liquid is absorbed. Add ½ cup of stock and stir for 3 to 5 minutes, until stock is absorbed. Repeat until all of the stock is used and rice is al dente but not under-cooked. If needed, add a little more stock to create a loose, fluid texture known as *all'onda*, which means wavy or "creating waves." Stir in the reserved corn and mushrooms, and the cheese. Season with salt and pepper. Keep warm.

GRILLED SALMON Preheat grill to high heat. Brush salmon with oil and season with salt and pepper.

Add salmon to the grill and cook for 3 minutes per side for medium-rare. Brush the tops with the BBQ sauce. Transfer salmon to a plate and set aside to rest 2 to 3 minutes.

ASSEMBLY Spoon risotto onto four deep plates. Arrange salmon beside it and drizzle a little BBQ sauce over the dish. Garnish with chopped herbs. Serve immediately.

CRISPY POLENTA
with Mushroom Bordelaise

CHEF: RYAN DONALDSON, GATHER KITCHEN & BAR

WINE PAIRING: Lauren Ashton Proprietor's Cuvée

You might expect a big, bold wine such as Lauren Ashton's cuvée to pair with traditional steak-house flavors, but this audacious mushroom bordelaise has all of the richness of a traditional demi-glace to stand up beautifully to the wine.

It's a great recipe to prepare ahead and put together at the last minute. You can make a large batch of the bordelaise and freeze it in ice-cube trays (one cube per portion). It's a delicious sauce for meatballs and steaks.

POLENTA CAKES Bring stock to a boil in a saucepan and season with salt and pepper. Gradually add polenta (or cornmeal), whisking continuously, until the polenta thickens. Reduce heat to low, cover, and cook for 30 to 40 minutes, stirring occasionally, until tender. Immediately transfer polenta to a greased baking sheet, spread out into an even ¾-inch-thick layer, and set aside to cool. Cover and refrigerate until needed.

MUSHROOM BORDELAISE Melt butter in a large skillet over medium heat. Add shallot and garlic and cook for 3 minutes, until soft and translucent. Add peppercorns, thyme, bay leaf, and wine. Reduce heat to medium and cook for 15 to 20 minutes, until the wine has reduced to a quarter of its original volume. Add apple juice and cook for another 10 to 15 minutes, until reduced by half. Stir in stock and cook for another 12 to 15 minutes, until a cup of stock remains. Season with salt and strain.

MUSHROOM CONSERVA Heat 1 tablespoon oil in a large saucepan over medium-high heat. Add shallot and garlic and cook for 1 minute, until garlic is fragrant and golden. Add tomato paste and cook for 2 minutes, stirring constantly.

POLENTA CAKES
4 cups vegetable stock
1 Tbsp kosher salt
1 tsp white pepper
1 cup yellow medium-ground polenta or cornmeal (preferably Bob's Red Mill) (see Note)

MUSHROOM BORDELAISE
1 Tbsp butter
1 shallot, finely chopped
2 cloves garlic, finely chopped
10 black peppercorns
3 sprigs thyme
1 bay leaf
2 cups red wine
1 cup apple juice
4 cups mushroom stock
Salt, to taste

MUSHROOM CONSERVA
1 cup + 1 Tbsp olive oil (divided)
1 large shallot, finely chopped
3 cloves garlic, thinly sliced
1 Tbsp tomato paste
¼ cup sherry vinegar
3 sprigs thyme
1 tsp kosher salt
1 tsp black pepper
1 lb mixed mushrooms

NOTE: Instant polenta can be used in a pinch, but it won't yield the same rich results.

Oil, for frying
Finishing salt and black
    pepper, to taste
4 eggs
2 oz chèvre (goat cheese)
    or fromage blanc
½ cup Mushroom Conserva
    (see here)
½ cup Mushroom Bordelaise
    (see here)
2 Tbsp chopped parsley,
    for garnish

Pour in vinegar, scraping the caramelized bits off the bottom of the pan, and cook for another 2 minutes, until it resembles a paste. Stir in remaining 1 cup oil. Add thyme, salt, and pepper and warm the oil until it begins to simmer. Add mushrooms, then immediately turn off the heat. Set aside for 1 hour to cool. Transfer to a mason jar until ready to use. (The mushroom conserva can be stored in the refrigerator for up to 1 month.)

ASSEMBLY Cut polenta into eight 3-inch squares. Cut them diagonally into triangles.

Add a ¼ inch of oil to a skillet over medium-high heat. Add polenta and fry for 3 minutes on each side, until golden brown. Transfer polenta to a paper-towel-lined plate to drain. Season with salt and pepper.

In the same skillet with the oil still hot, fry the eggs for 1 minute over high heat.

Place a dollop of chèvre (or fromage blanc) in the center of each plate and arrange four triangles of polenta on top, slightly overlapped. Place an egg on top of the polenta.

Using a slotted spoon, place mushrooms in a skillet set over medium-high heat. Add bordelaise and bring to a simmer. Remove from heat immediately and spoon mushrooms over eggs and polenta. Garnish with parsley and black pepper and serve immediately.

L'ECOLE
N° 41

+

MARTY
CLUBB

It's been said that behind every successful small business is a family, and L'Ecole N° 41 is no exception. The artisan winery was founded in 1983 by Jean and Baker Ferguson. While they were starting up the winery, their daughter Megan and her husband, Marty, would come up from San Francisco to help with the fall harvest. And in 1989, Megan and Marty made a permanent move to Walla Walla to run the family business.

In fact, Marty, who is now the winemaker, often jokes that he tripped headfirst into winemaking and married his way into the business. His first introduction to wine was from his father-in-law. "Before I met Megan, I didn't know what wine was!" Marty muses. But as a chemical engineer, he had a background that suited the role. "Much of winemaking is chemistry," he explains. "And because we were living in the Bay Area, I started taking classes at UC Davis,

dove in, and started doing it." But the new role of winemaker came with its own challenges. "It was me, myself, and I for four years, and it paid nothing. My happiest moment was finally hiring someone to help."

Marty's style of winemaking is one of minimal intervention, and "as clean, expressive, and balanced as [we] can make them." This subtle style of winemaking—from a team who wants to produce balanced, food-friendly, and age-worthy wines—hasn't gone unnoticed. L'Ecole N° 41 has been regarded as a Top 100 Winery in the world by *Wine & Spirits* magazine fifteen times, their Estate Perigee has wrangled gold medals

from *Decanter* magazine, and their 2011 Estate Ferguson Vineyard earned the prestigious 2014 international trophy for "Best in Show Red Bordeaux Varietal over £15."

"We adopt new technologies, but at the end of the day, we like to do things traditionally," Marty shares, adding, "You might say we're old-school." For a winery that's named after an old school-house and the school district where it's located, the comment seems perfectly fitting.

BLACK-COD "TOFU"

with Sticky Soy CHEF: MAXIMILLIAN PETTY,

EDEN HILL RESTAURANT AND EDEN HILL PROVISIONS

SERVES 6 TO 8
(AS AN APPETIZER)

1 lb fresh skinless black cod fillets, cut into ½-inch cubes
5 tsp kosher salt
5 tsp granulated sugar
4 eggs
½ cup + 2 Tbsp heavy cream
6½ fl oz good brandy
½ cup (1 stick) + 1 Tbsp melted butter, warmed
1 loaf brioche, cut into ⅛-inch pieces
3 Tbsp clarified butter, warmed (divided)
Kecap manis, for garnish
Mixed herbs, such as chives, parley, cilantro, and dill, chopped, for garnish

WINE PAIRING: L'Ecole N° 41 Chenin Blanc

This simple appetizer sees steamed black-cod tofu on a slice of lightly toasted brioche. The sticky soy is made with *kecap manis*—a sweet and thick soy sauce that can be found at Asian food markets.

When it comes to wine pairing, a white wine such as L'Ecole N° 41's Chenin Blanc has good acidity and intensity to complement the sweet and savory characteristics of this dish.

In a food processor, combine black cod, salt, and sugar and process for 30 seconds. Add eggs, cream, brandy, and melted butter and purée until smooth. Press mixture through a tamis or fine-mesh strainer, straining out impurities.

On a piece of parchment paper, spread out mixture into three 3-inch squares about ¾ inch deep. Carefully place the parchment paper with the mixture into a steamer set over simmering water and steam for 14 minutes. Remove from steamer and refrigerate until cooled.

Once cool, cut each square into three 1- × 3-inch pieces. Cut the brioche slices into the same shape as your "tofu." Using a kitchen brush, paint brioche and "tofu" together with 2 tablespoons of the clarified butter. Set aside to cool so the butter hardens.

Heat the remaining 1 tablespoon of clarified butter in a skillet over medium heat. Add the black cod bread-side down and toast for 1 minute, until golden and crispy. Remove, and flip onto the plate bread-side up. Drizzle with kecap manis and garnish with herbs.

ASPARAGUS AND SMOKED HAZELNUT TART

with Black-Garlic Dressing CHEF: MAXIMILLIAN PETTY,

EDEN HILL RESTAURANT AND EDEN HILL PROVISIONS

BLACK-GARLIC DRESSING
4 cloves black garlic (see Note)
2 egg yolks
1 cup good-quality olive oil
½ cup aged balsamic vinegar
2 Tbsp wildflower honey
½ tsp black pepper
Salt, to taste

ASPARAGUS TART
1 cup (2 sticks) butter, room
   temperature, plus extra for
   greasing or use cooking spray
½ cup granulated sugar
1¾ cups all-purpose flour
½ cup almond flour
½ cup hazelnuts, toasted,
   peeled, and ground
2 tsp kosher salt
4 eggs
1 lb asparagus, trimmed
   and ends peeled
1 egg yolk, lightly beaten
   (optional)
6 raw egg yolks, whole (optional)

NOTE: Black garlic can
be purchased in Asian
food markets, but you
can also make your
own. Place heads of
garlic in a rice cooker
or slow cooker on the
"keep warm" setting
and slowly cook for
14 days.

WINE PAIRING: L'Ecole N° 41 Estate Perigee

This beautiful tart sings spring, especially when prepared with
fresh young asparagus. It may come as a surprise that we've
paired this dish with a bigger red wine, but it works well.
The black garlic—sweet and anise-like with hints of fragrant
cardamom and tamarind—brings out the complex notes in
this elegant, well-structured wine.

BLACK-GARLIC DRESSING Combine all ingredients in a
blender and mix until emulsified. (Leftover dressing can be
stored in an airtight container in the refrigerator for up to
7 days.)

ASPARAGUS TART Preheat oven to 400°F.

In a stand mixer fitted with a paddle attachment, cream
butter and sugar on medium-high speed for 1 minute. Add
flours, hazelnuts, and salt and mix on low speed for 30 seconds. Add eggs one at a time. Transfer mixture into a piping
bag with a large round tip. Set aside.

Bring a saucepan of salted water to a boil. Add asparagus
and cook for 3 minutes. Drain, then transfer asparagus to a
bowl of ice water to cool.

Grease six 4-inch tart pans with butter (or cooking
spray). Drain the asparagus, then trim an inch off the stalks
so that the lengths are even. Arrange asparagus in the
tart pans and pipe an even layer of dough on top. Bake for
12 minutes, until golden and a cake tester comes out clean.
Remove, flip over, and drizzle with fresh egg yolk, if using.
(Alternatively, place a raw egg yolk on top.)

Transfer tart to a serving plate and drizzle black-garlic
dressing on top.

LOCUS WINES

+

RICH BURTON

As the saying goes, retirement is when you stop living at work and start working at living. And for Rich Burton, his post-tech job plan was always to run a winery with his business and life partner, Ton Yazici. "We were frequently traveling to places such as Champagne and Burgundy and realized that we were building our lives around vacations to wine regions."

Having built careers in the corporate world, they believed a winery would serve as a creative outlet. "Rather than quit our jobs and go all in, we were smart about it," says Rich. He enrolled in WSU's enology program and began experimenting with winemaking on the side. "The chemistry behind winemaking was new to me, since the last time I needed to understand chemistry was in high school." Rich and Ton turned their dream into reality when they opened Locus Wines in 2011. They sourced fruit from upstart vineyards, rented space in a winemaking facility, joined a cooperative tasting room in Seattle's Post Alley, and eventually established their own tasting room in Pioneer Square.

The men are self-professed Europhiles with a love for Old World wines. "On those trips, the wines we were drinking on a daily basis were European wines under twenty dollars, and we don't see a lot of that in Washington." So Rich focuses on his favorite Rhône varieties that best champion Washington's native climate and soil.

Rich relies heavily on Ton's culinary education, passion, and experience to craft wines with good acidity that pair well with food. Their 2013 Syrah-Grenache is the perfect example of a medium-bodied Rhône-style blend, with a lush bouquet of candied strawberries, plums, and herbs and a hint of coffee and vanilla.

Ultimately, these are wines that inspired Rich in the first place: affordable, easy-to-drink, and well suited to accompany a midweek meal or to enjoy on their own. "We are not in this to make fifty-dollar bottles of wine," he shares. "Instead, we make wines that people can and want to drink every day." Cheers to that, or as they say in France, À *votre santé!*

MINTED GREEN GARBANZO AND BURRATA TOAST

COURTESY OF SONI DAVE-SCHOCK, CO-OWNER OF BOTTLEHOUSE

GREEN GARBANZO MASH

3 lbs green garbanzo beans, shelled (yields 4 cups)
Grated zest and juice of 3 lemons
3 cloves garlic
⅓ cup mint leaves
1 cup extra-virgin olive oil
Salt and black pepper, to taste

ASSEMBLY

1 bâtard or Campagne loaf
Extra-virgin olive oil, for drizzling
4 (4-oz) fresh burrata balls, cut into 4 slices
Grated lemon zest, for garnish
2 cups microgreens, for garnish
Finishing salt, for sprinkling

WINE PAIRING: Locus Rosé

Fresh, protein-packed green garbanzo beans—which are just garbanzo beans harvested early—can be found at farmers' markets late spring through the summer. They come available either in their natural husk or shelled, so be sure to account for time and yield when preparing this recipe.

The Locus Wines rosé balances fresh acidity with an abundance of stone fruit and fresh herbal notes. Alongside this recipe, it highlights the herbal notes of the garbanzo mash, and the wine's racy acidity is balanced with the fattiness of the burrata. Together, the two create an expression of summer abundance.

GREEN GARBANZO MASH Bring a saucepan of salted water to a boil over high heat. Add garbanzo beans and cook for 2 to 3 minutes, or until soft. Drain, then transfer to a bowl of ice water. Let sit in ice water for 4 to 5 minutes. Drain.

In a food processor, combine garbanzo beans, lemon zest and juice, garlic, and mint. Pulse until combined yet coarse. With the motor running, gradually pour in oil until it has a hummus-like consistency. Season to taste with salt and pepper.

Refrigerate if not using immediately. (Leftover mash can be covered and stored in an airtight container in the refrigerator for up to 2 days.)

ASSEMBLY Preheat grill or broiler to high heat.

Trim off ends of loaf, then cut into eight slices 1 inch thick. Toast bread for 1 to 2 minutes, until lightly browned. Remove from the grill or oven and drizzle with oil.

Spread ⅓ cup of green garbanzo mash over each slice of toast. Arrange two slices of burrata on top of each. Cut toast in half, then top with lemon zest, microgreens, and salt. Serve immediately.

OXTAIL RILLETTES with
Apricot Mostarda and Pickled Red Onion

COURTESY OF HENRI SCHOCK, CO-OWNER OF BOTTLEHOUSE

MAKES 5 (6-OZ) JARS

WINE PAIRING: Locus Red

A rillette, not unlike a pâté, is commonly made with chopped meat that is heavily salted and slowly cooked in fat. This silky-smooth oxtail version is ideal for a dinner party served on a platter alongside baguettes, cheese, and pickles. Alternatively, it can be spread on toast and served with a fresh salad for a light meal.

We've paired it with Locus Wines' smooth and restrained Rhône-style blend that has the structure and spice to enhance the flavors of this dish. Silky and fatty, the oxtail rillettes are a necessary supplement to the cooler-climate, acid-rich fruit featured in this wine.

APRICOT MOSTARDA Combine sugar and ⅓ cup water in a medium saucepan. Bring to a boil over medium heat, stirring until the sugar is dissolved. Remove from heat and cool slightly.

Add apricots and wine and simmer over medium heat for 15 minutes, until apricots are softened.

Transfer apricots to a bowl and stir in mustard, chili flakes, and oil and set aside to cool completely. Place in an airtight container in the refrigerator overnight before using. (Mostarda can be stored in the refrigerator for up to 1 month.)

OXTAIL RILLETTES Heat oil in a large, heavy-bottomed Dutch oven set over medium-high heat. Add oxtails and brown on all sides. Transfer oxtails to a plate and set aside.

Add shallot and celery to the pan and sauté over medium heat for 10 minutes, until well browned. Add cumin seeds and toast for 2 to 3 minutes, until fragrant. Add Dijon and combine until fully incorporated. Pour in wine and orange juice.

APRICOT MOSTARDA
⅓ cup granulated sugar
½ lb dried apricots, chopped
¼ cup dry white wine
1 Tbsp mustard seeds
1 tsp chili flakes
½ Tbsp extra-virgin olive oil

OXTAIL RILLETTES
1 Tbsp vegetable oil
5 lbs oxtail, cut into 2-inch segments (ask your butcher)
1 shallot, thinly sliced
1 stalk celery, roughly chopped
½ Tbsp cumin seeds
½ cup Dijon mustard
½ (750-ml) bottle white wine
½ cup orange juice
2 large sprigs thyme
1 Tbsp black peppercorns
2 cups bacon fat
Grated zest of 1 large orange

½ cup apple cider vinegar
1 Tbsp honey
½ Tbsp kosher salt
1 red onion, thinly sliced

ASSEMBLY
Baguette, sliced, to serve
Cornichons, to serve

Return oxtails to the pan, then add thyme and peppercorns. Cover and simmer over low heat for 4 to 6 hours, until the meat falls off the bone. Remove the oxtails and set aside to cool. Pick meat off the bone. Strain stock and refrigerate for at least 4 hours or overnight. The cooled stock will form a fat cap, which should be reserved. (Discard the stock.)

Heat bacon fat and oxtail fat cap in a large skillet over medium-high heat. Cook until fully melted. Set aside and keep warm.

In 6-ounce jars, tightly pack 4 ounces of oxtail meat. Top each with 1 to 2 tablespoons of melted fat and garnish with orange zest. Chill in the refrigerator until fat is set.

PICKLED RED ONION In a small bowl, combine vinegar, honey, salt, and 1 cup water. Whisk ingredients together until dissolved.

Place onion in a jar or airtight container and add pickling liquid. Set aside at room temperature for 1 hour. This recipe can be made 2 weeks prior if covered and chilled.

ASSEMBLY Bring oxtail rillettes to room temperature, about 30 to 45 minutes. Place the apricot mostarda and pickled red onion in small bowls and arrange on a large platter. Serve with baguette and cornichons.

LODMELL CELLARS

+

KRISTIE LODMELL

As the great-granddaughter of a four-generation wheat farming family, Kristie Lodmell traded a life in biotechnology for a return to her roots.

In the late 1880s, Kristie's great-grandfather William Struthers planted wheat on a piece of land by the lower Snake River, which is now home to Lodmell Vineyards (the Lodmell wine label features a coiled snake). What started as a fifteen-acre plot of grapevines has now expanded to thirty acres of Cabernet Sauvignon, Merlot, Cabernet Franc, Syrah, and Sémillon. These days, Kristie and her father, Miles, work the vineyards together.

The family planted the vineyard in 1997 and began selling fruit to award-winning winemakers, such as Woodward Canyon's Rick Small, who, in return, introduced Kristie's brother Andrew to winemaking. Andrew opened Lodmell Cellars in 2005 with a focus on Bordeaux-style estate wines, with

his first commercial vintage being Merlot, Lodmell's flagship (and award-winning) varietal.

Kristie was appointed general manager and partner in 2008 and worked with Andrew before taking over the winery and winemaking duties completely in 2016. She reveals that one of the best things about the winery is having complete control over the grapes. "Our wines are well received by consumers and critics because the estate fruit is consistent," says Kristie. "The vineyard was planted on unique terroir in Walla Walla County, and with natural rainfall of less than eight inches per year augmented by irrigation, it allows us to control moisture."

As a result, the plants form tight clusters and produce small, intensely fruity grapes. Sublime, a blend of Merlot, Cabernet Sauvignon, and Carménère, won a Double Gold medal at the 2017 Seattle Wine Awards and received platinum status by *Wine Press Northwest*.

Kristie has come full circle, from bench research to corporate America to Lodmell Cellars. "I'm applying my scientific skills in the lab, creating and blending my final products, and I am proud to be part of the Washington wine industry."

You can find the Lodmell Cellars tasting room inside the historic Marcus Whitman Hotel in Walla Walla.

SASHIMI SCALLOPS, Soy-Miso
Vinaigrette, Wasabi Aioli, and Pickled Ginger

CHEF: CHAD BOSTWICK, WALLA WALLA STEAK CO.

SOY-MISO VINAIGRETTE

1 clove garlic, chopped
1 tsp grated ginger
1 tsp finely chopped chives
¾ tsp black pepper
⅓ cup soy sauce
⅓ cup rice vinegar
2½ Tbsp red miso paste
1 cup canola oil

WASABI AIOLI

¼ cup high-quality mayonnaise
½ Tbsp wasabi powder
½ Tbsp granulated sugar
1 tsp seasoned rice vinegar

ASSEMBLY

8 scallop shells, halved, for plating
16 sashimi-grade scallops
1 cup Soy-Miso Vinaigrette
  (see here)
¼ cup Wasabi Aioli (see here)
2 to 3 slices pickled ginger,
  julienned

WINE PAIRING: Lodmell Sauvignon Blanc

This summertime crowd-pleaser is one of Walla Walla Steak Co.'s most popular appetizers. It's cold, crisp, and refreshing with bright, delicate flavors.

Lodmell Cellars' Sauvignon Blanc is beautiful on its own, but this dish of fresh scallops highlights the wine's complex notes. And with a burst of umami flavor from the vinaigrette and a powerful punch of wasabi aioli to the finish, it's an extraordinary orchestra of flavors to excite the palate.

SOY-MISO VINAIGRETTE Combine all ingredients except the oil in a blender and blend until smooth. With the motor running, gradually pour in oil and blend until emulsified. Set aside.

WASABI AIOLI In a small bowl, combine all ingredients.

ASSEMBLY Place scallop shells on a bed of ice. Place two scallops on each shell. Pour vinaigrette around the scallop, then top with wasabi aioli and garnish with one or two strips of pickled ginger.

VEGETARIAN LASAGNA

CHEF: CHAD BOSTWICK, WALLA WALLA STEAK CO.

BÉCHAMEL SAUCE

2 Tbsp butter
½ small onion, finely chopped
2 Tbsp all-purpose flour
½ tsp kosher salt, plus extra to taste
4 cups whole milk

VEGETARIAN LASAGNA

2 zucchinis, cut into ¼-inch-thick slices
2 yellow squash, cut into ¼-inch-thick slices
1 eggplant, cut into ¼-inch-thick slices
Salt, for sprinkling vegetables
Olive oil, for drizzling
2 Tbsp olive oil
1 onion, finely chopped (1 cup)
2 cups cremini mushrooms, sliced
3 cloves garlic, finely chopped
1 lb fresh spinach
2 cups ricotta
2 eggs
Salt and black pepper, to taste
4 cups tomato sauce
Parcooked lasagna sheets for 3 (9- × 13-inch) layers
6 cups shredded mozzarella
1 cup chopped canned artichoke hearts
1 cup grated Parmesan
1 quantity Béchamel Sauce (see here)
½ cup chopped parsley

WINE PAIRING: Lodmell Sublime

A bold flavorsome dish like this requires an equally confident wine. Lodmell Cellars' Sublime—a well-balanced and nuanced blend of Merlot, Cabernet Sauvignon, and Carménère—makes a notable impression and completes the meal.

BÉCHAMEL SAUCE Melt butter in a saucepan over medium heat. Add onion and cook for 6 minutes, until softened. Add flour and salt and cook for another 5 minutes, until golden and nutty. Gradually whisk in milk and mix until smooth. Stir and bring to a boil. Reduce heat to medium-low and simmer, stirring occasionally, for 10 minutes, until thickened. Season with salt. Strain through a fine-mesh strainer.

VEGETARIAN LASAGNA Preheat oven to 400°F.

Season zucchinis, squash, and eggplant with salt and arrange on two baking sheets, keeping the eggplant separate. Drizzle with oil and roast for 8 to 10 minutes, until edges begin to brown. Remove from the oven, then set aside to cool.

Heat oil in a large skillet over medium-high heat. Add onion and mushrooms and cook for 3 minutes, until onion is translucent. Add garlic and cook for another minute, until fragrant. Add spinach and cook for another 1 to 2 minutes, until wilted. Drain mixture and set aside to cool.

In a large bowl, combine the spinach mixture, ricotta, and eggs, then season with salt and pepper.

In a 9- × 13-inch baking pan, spread a thin, even layer of tomato sauce on the bottom. Add lasagna sheets to cover the entire pan, then add another thin, even layer of tomato sauce and a handful of mozzarella.

Add a layer of roasted zucchini and squash, then tomato sauce, half the mozzarella, and lasagna sheets.

Add a layer of spinach mixture, then cover with roasted eggplant. Add tomato sauce, the remaining mozzarella, squash, and lasagna sheets.

Add artichokes and Parmesan. Pour in béchamel and bake for 40 to 50 minutes, until the béchamel is golden brown and the center is hot. Garnish with parsley.

MARK RYAN WINERY

+

MARK RYAN MCNEILLY

He has one of the most recognizable names when it comes to Washington wine, which is impressive considering his foray into winemaking was purely by chance. Mark Ryan McNeilly was working for a wine distributor when he discovered the expansive range of wines available to him. "I was tasting four-dollar wines from Chile and $500 wines from Burgundy. Understanding the wine spectrum was exciting."

Mark began to produce wines out of his garage in 1999. He had no formal winemaking training, other than a weekend course at UC Davis to learn chemical analysis. "I read as many books as I could get my hands on and talked to winemakers from all over the world." And Jim Holmes, who is now the owner of Ciel du Cheval Vineyard, was his greatest mentor.

Mark moved into his own facility in Woodinville in 2003. In 2012, he opened a second tasting room in Walla Walla. Today, his winery controls almost eighty acres of Washington vineyard, mostly in Red Mountain. And because Red Mountain grapes are inherently fruit dominant, coaxing a little softness into his wines is essential for Mark. "We want both power and elegance however we get there!"

Long Haul Merlot and Dead Horse Cabernet Sauvignon are two flagship wines. "People are drawn to wines with tons of New World fruit and a little Old World structure, and these two wines illustrate that nicely."

Mark Ryan Winery produces forty-five thousand cases of wine a year, placing them in the top twenty-five for winery size out of the nearly one thousand wineries currently in Washington state.

"When I first started in 1999, I thought I had totally missed the wave of wineries that opened in Woodinville around that time. When people ask me today if they should start a winery, my answer is a definite yes. There are still great opportunities in Washington."

BEEF TENDERLOIN
with Corn and Chanterelles

CHEF: ETHAN STOWELL, ETHAN STOWELL RESTAURANTS

SERVES 4

2 cups red wine
2 Tbsp butter
2 cup fresh corn kernels
2 cups small chanterelle
  mushrooms, quartered
1 Tbsp finely chopped shallot
1 Tbsp chopped parsley
Salt and black pepper, to taste
2 Tbsp olive oil
4 (6-oz) center-cut beef
  tenderloins
1 cup demi-glace (see Note)
1 Tbsp thyme leaves

NOTE: Demi-glace (veal glaze) is a gourmet item that can be found at fine food stores or via Amazon. Alternatively, use a premium beef base (located in the soup and stock aisle of supermarkets) and thicken with a little cornstarch.

WINE PAIRING: Mark Ryan Dead Horse

This heavyweight dish demands a hearty Washington red to do it justice. Mark Ryan's Dead Horse is a Red Mountain Cabernet, bolstered by a healthy dose of new French oak that offers depth and power to spare. Bramble fruit and baking spice mingle with the beef, corn, and chanterelles, while the earthy and peppered minerality provide a complex lingering backdrop.

Heat wine in a saucepan over medium heat and simmer for 5 minutes, until it's reduced by half and coats the back of a spoon. Set aside.

Heat butter in a skillet over medium heat. Add corn and mushrooms and cook for 4 to 5 minutes, until released liquids have evaporated. Add shallot and parsley and season with salt and pepper. Keep warm.

Preheat oven to 400°F.

Heat oil in a large ovenproof skillet over medium-high heat, until the oil begins to smoke. Season steaks with salt and pepper and add them to the pan. Sear for 2 to 3 minutes on each side, until brown and crispy. Transfer pan to the oven and cook for 4 to 5 minutes for medium-rare to medium. Remove pan from the oven and place the steaks on a platter to rest for 6 to 8 minutes.

Heat the wine syrup and demi-glace in a small saucepan and season to taste with salt and pepper. Spoon the corn and chanterelle mixture on four warm plates and arrange a steak on each. Add thyme to the sauce and spoon over the steaks. Serve immediately.

HALIBUT with Asparagus, Maitake Mushrooms, Green Garlic, and Porcini Brodo

CHEF: ETHAN STOWELL, ETHAN STOWELL RESTAURANTS

SERVES 4

WINE PAIRING: Mark Ryan Chardonnay

This full-bodied Chardonnay brims with citrus, apple, and melon, which work well with the subtle sweetness of halibut. There's also just enough new oak to stand up to the asparagus and earthy maitake mushrooms. It's a complex dish that marries perfectly on the palate.

MAITAKE MUSHROOMS Preheat oven to 450°F.

In a bowl, combine maitake, oil, and salt and pepper and toss until mushrooms are evenly coated. Transfer mushrooms to a baking sheet and spread out in a single layer. Roast for 10 to 15 minutes, until golden brown. Set aside.

GREEN GARLIC Melt butter in a medium saucepan over low heat. Add green garlic and sweat for 10 to 15 minutes, until translucent and tender. Season with salt and pepper.

PORCINI BRODO Heat oil in a stockpot over medium-high heat. Add carrot, celery, fennel, onion, maitake stems, and green garlic ends and cook for 10 minutes, until vegetables are caramelized. Add porcini along with the soaking liquid, thyme, bay leaves, and salt and pepper. Cover with water and bring to a boil. Reduce heat to medium and simmer, uncovered, for 1 hour.

Strain into a clean saucepan and simmer over medium heat until reduced by half. Season with salt and pepper.

ASSEMBLY Heat 2 tablespoons oil in a large skillet over medium-high heat. Season halibut on both sides with salt and pepper. Add fish to the pan flesh-side down and cook for 4 minutes, until golden brown. Flip fish and cook for another 3 minutes, until the fish is warm in the center.

Heat the remaining tablespoon of oil in a skillet over high heat. Add maitake mushrooms and asparagus and sauté for 3 to 4 minutes, until warmed through. Reheat green garlic in a small skillet.

Ladle porcini brodo into four shallow bowls. Divide green garlic, maitake and asparagus among the bowls. Arrange a piece of halibut on top of the maitake and asparagus. Finish with salt and drizzle olive oil on top.

MAITAKE MUSHROOMS
4 oz maitake mushrooms, trimmed and cut into wedges (stems reserved)
2 Tbsp olive oil
Salt and black pepper, to taste

GREEN GARLIC
½ cup (1 stick) butter
½ lb green garlic (spring garlic or young garlic), cleaned and thinly sliced (green ends reserved for the brodo)
Salt and black pepper, to taste

PORCINI BRODO
¼ cup olive oil
1 large carrot, diced
2 stalks celery, diced
1 bulb fennel, diced
1 onion, diced
Reserved maitake stems
Reserved green garlic ends, chopped
4 oz dried porcini mushrooms, soaked in 4 cups hot water for 20 to 30 minutes
Small bunch of thyme
4 to 6 bay leaves
Salt and black pepper, to taste

ASSEMBLY
3 Tbsp olive oil (divided)
4 (4-oz) portions fresh halibut, skin on
Salt and black pepper, to taste
½ lb asparagus, cut diagonally ¼ inch thick
Finishing salt, for sprinkling
Extra-virgin olive oil, for drizzling

MARYHILL WINERY

+

RICHARD BATCHELOR

Growing up in the beautiful countryside of New Zealand, Richard Batchelor became interested in horticulture at a young age. His dad used the family farm for food, made wine and beer as a side hobby, and was an avid diver, so there was always fresh seafood, meat, preserves, and vegetables on the table. And, yes, Richard had his first taste of wine at a young age.

As he got older, he became interested in viticulture and enology, which ultimately led him to winemaking. "I find winemaking a little more fun and exciting than growing grapes," says Richard, who moved to the Sonoma Valley from New Zealand in 2000 as part of an exchange program. After a decade of working for California wineries, Richard moved to the Columbia Gorge to work for Maryhill Winery. Washington state offered him exposure and access to a diversity of grape-growing regions.

Historically, Maryhill was traditional in its wine varieties, known for Zinfandel, Cabernet, and Viognier. Since Richard has come on board, they're producing a lot more Spanish and Italian varieties, like Carménère, Mourvèdre, and Albariño. "We have thirty-one varieties. There's a big diversity of grapes there. Looking after all those little babies all the way through—I have fun with that."

Located at the eastern end of the Columbia Gorge, Maryhill can grow warmer grapes, like Cabernet and Zinfandel. "Growing Zin is really challenging. With any exposure to moisture, rain, and humidity, it will rot very quickly. Because our climate is dry and we

have the wind factor, any rain will dry up quickly."

Maryhill wines are soft and approachable. "It's nice to produce a few wines that need to age five to ten years before they can be enjoyed, but we want people to come to the tasting room, enjoy the wines straightaway, and then take home a bottle to drink that night with friends."

CHARCOAL-ROASTED BEETS

with Chèvre Ajo Blanco, Hazelnuts, and Herb Salad CHEF: AARON TEKULVE, SURRELL

SERVES 4 TO 6

CHÈVRE AJO BLANCO

1 Tbsp butter
1 large shallot, chopped (¼ cup)
2 to 3 cloves garlic, chopped
   (1 Tbsp)
¼ cup salted hazelnuts, toasted
½ cup dry white wine
½ cup chèvre (goat cheese)
½ cup heavy cream
¼ cup white wine vinegar, plus
   extra to taste
Salt, to taste

CHARCOAL-ROASTED BEETS

10 lbs lump (hardwood)
   charcoal (do not use charcoal
   briquettes)
10 beets, unpeeled and washed
½ cup grapeseed or rice bran oil
1 large shallot, finely chopped
   (¼ cup)
¾ cup fruity extra-virgin olive oil
   (preferably Arbequina)
¼ cup sherry vinegar, plus extra
   to taste
Salt and black pepper, to taste

HERB SALAD

1 cup baby arugula
¼ cup chopped basil
¼ cup chopped dill
2 Tbsp chopped tarragon
Salt and black pepper, to taste

ASSEMBLY

1 cup crumbled chèvre, for
   garnish
1 cup salted hazelnuts, toasted
   and chopped, for garnish

WINE PAIRING: Maryhill Proprietor's Reserve Zinfandel

Chef Aaron Tekulve grew up eating beets in late fall when they are packed with flavor. Here, they're beautifully plated with chèvre ajo blanco (traditionally, a chilled Spanish soup), hazelnuts, and fresh herbs. The earthiness and subtle sweetness of the Zinfandel truly complement these ingredients.

CHÈVRE AJO BLANCO Heat butter in a saucepan over medium heat. Add shallot and garlic and sauté for 1 to 2 minutes, until softened but not caramelized. Stir in hazelnuts, then pour in wine. Cook for 3 to 5 minutes, until reduced by a third.

Add chèvre, cream, and vinegar and cook for 3 to 5 minutes, until chèvre has melted and hazelnuts have softened. Transfer mixture to a blender and purée until smooth. Season with salt and more vinegar. The sauce should have a yogurt-like consistency. If needed, thin it out with water.

CHARCOAL-ROASTED BEETS Preheat oven to 400°F. Heat the charcoal in your grill until coals are hot. (You can use a chimney starter to get it going faster.)

In a large bowl, combine beets and grapeseed (or rice bran) oil and toss. Using tongs, place beets into the hot embers and rotate every 5 to 7 minutes, until all sides are charred. (A total of 20 to 25 minutes.) Transfer beets to a roasting pan and place a few large pieces of charcoal on top. Carefully wrap pan in aluminum foil and roast for 30 to 45 minutes, until beets can be pierced with a knife. Carefully transfer charcoal into the grill.

Using a dish towel, rub off skin. Use a vegetable peeler to remove any remaining skin. Set aside to cool, then cut beets into 2-inch pieces and put them into a bowl. Add shallot, olive oil, and vinegar and toss. Season with salt and pepper.

HERB SALAD In a bowl, combine all ingredients and toss.

ASSEMBLY Add a smear of chèvre ajo blanco to a large serving platter. Arrange beets on top, then garnish with chèvre, hazelnuts, and herb salad.

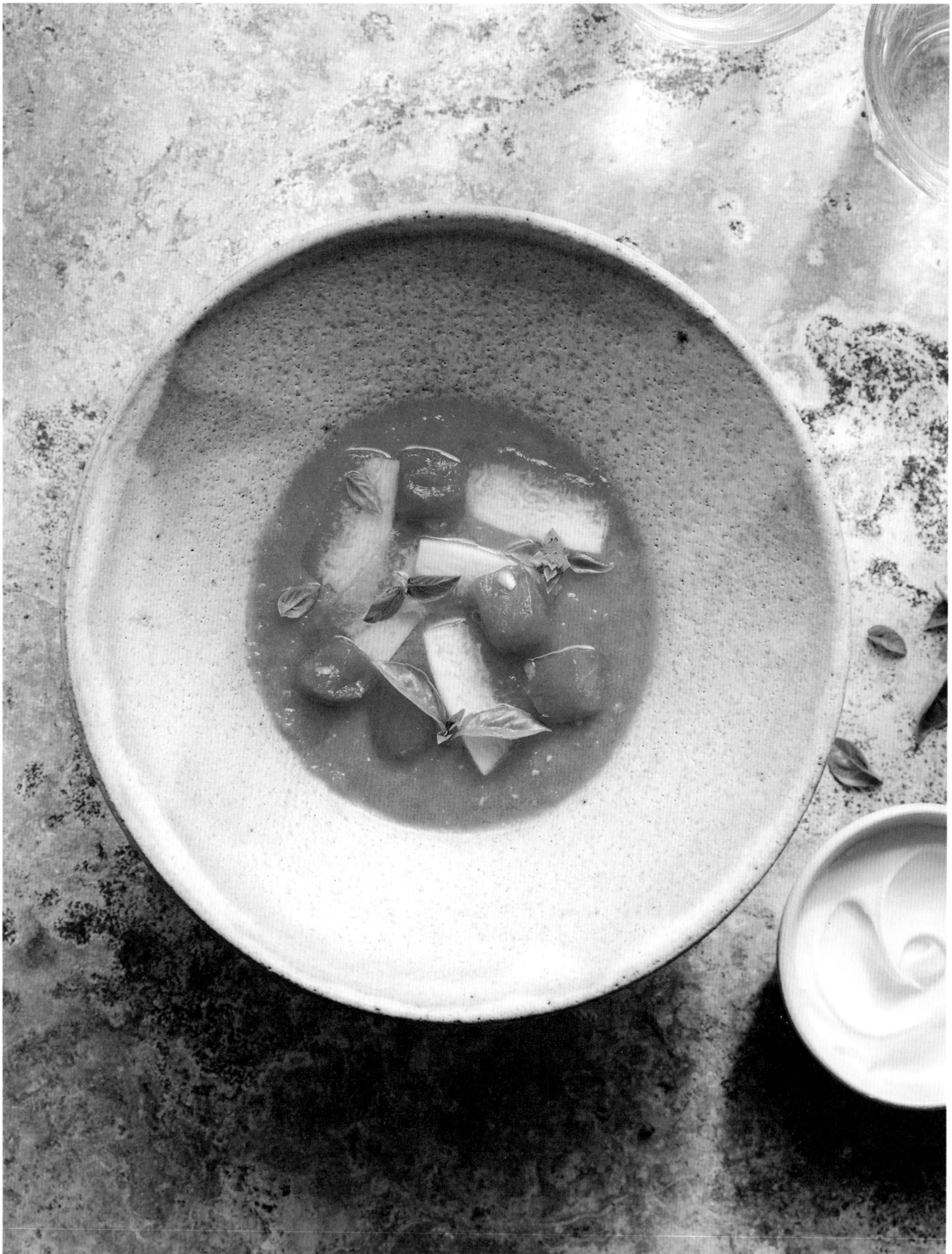

Tomato and Watermelon Gazpacho | p. 168

TOMATO AND WATERMELON GAZPACHO

CHEF: AARON TEKULVE, SURRELL

Pictured p. 166

SERVES 4

WINE PAIRING: Maryhill Proprietor's Reserve Albariño

Gazpacho is a great expression of tomatoes, peppers, and even watermelon. With the sharpness of vinegar and creamy crème fraîche, this summer soup is equally luxurious and exciting to eat. The hint of strawberry in Maryhill's Albariño speaks to summer as much as this soup does.

PICKLED WATERMELON RINDS In a small saucepan, combine all ingredients except the watermelon, and bring to a simmer over high heat. Remove and set aside to cool to room temperature.

Using a knife, carefully cut 1 inch off the top and bottom of the watermelon to expose the flesh, then stand watermelon upright. Using a sawing motion, cut the skin of the melon where the white meets the green part. (You are peeling the watermelon but intentionally keeping the white rind on.) Discard green peels. Using the same sawing motion, cut off the white rind. Reserve the flesh.

Shape the rinds into large rectangles, then cut them into 1- × ⅛-inch matchsticks. Place rinds in a nonreactive container and pour the cooled pickling liquid over the top. Cover and refrigerate for at least 24 hours. The pickled rinds can be stored in the refrigerator for up to 2 months. (Makes 4 cups.)

MARINATED WATERMELON In a small bowl, combine all ingredients except the watermelon, and whisk. Place watermelon in a large ziplock bag in a uniform layer and pour in the marinade. Seal bag, removing as much air as possible. Turn over bag to coat watermelon. Refrigerate for at least a few hours but preferably overnight, rotating at least three to four times. (Makes 2 cups.)

PICKLED WATERMELON RINDS
2 large cloves garlic, crushed
1 bay leaf
2 tsp kosher salt
1 tsp granulated sugar
1 cup white wine vinegar
1 large seedless watermelon

MARINATED WATERMELON
¼ cup aged soy sauce
¼ cup lime juice
Grated zest of 1 lime
2 Tbsp fish sauce
1 shallot, finely chopped
1 tsp garlic paste or grated garlic
1 tsp kosher salt
2 cups cubed watermelon

TOMATO AND WATERMELON GAZPACHO

2 Tbsp olive oil

4 large shallots, roughly chopped (1 cup)

4 large cloves garlic, chopped

3 Tbsp fish sauce

2 Tbsp aged soy sauce

3 ripe heirloom tomatoes (about 1½ lbs), roughly chopped

3 cups chopped watermelon

¼ cup red wine vinegar, plus extra to taste

½ cup extra-virgin olive oil, plus extra for drizzling

Salt and black pepper, to taste

1 quantity Marinated Watermelon (see here)

1 cup crème fraîche

½ cup Pickled Watermelon Rinds (see here)

1 cup basil leaves, torn into ½-inch pieces

TOMATO AND WATERMELON GAZPACHO Heat the 2 tablespoons of oil in a small saucepan over low heat. Add shallot and garlic and sauté for 2 to 3 minutes, until softened. Transfer mixture to a blender, then add fish sauce, soy sauce, tomatoes, watermelon, and vinegar and blend until smooth.

With the motor running on medium-high speed, gradually pour in the ½ cup extra-virgin olive oil. The soup should have the consistency of heavy cream. If necessary, thin it out with a little water. Season to taste with salt and pepper and more vinegar until the soup is slightly acidic. Refrigerate until chilled.

Ladle soup into bowls. Garnish with five pieces of marinated watermelon, then drizzle with oil. Add a dollop of crème fraîche to the center of the bowl and finish with pickled watermelon rinds and basil.

MATTHEWS WINERY

+

ARYN MORELL

Bordeaux inspired, Washington crafted . . . It's a fitting tagline for Matthews Winery, which, since 1992, has been crafting delicious Bordeaux-style blends from Cabernet Sauvignon, Merlot, Cabernet Franc, Malbec, and Petit Verdot, and white wines exclusively from Sauvignon Blanc and Sémillon. The family-owned and -operated winery may take a cue from the wine-blending techniques of France's best-known wine region to show its appreciation of Old World traditions, but Matthews Winery wines are clearly rooted in the soils of Washington state.

The region is actually home to a number of diverse microclimates, each one providing its own unique terroir. Matthews' wines show balance, structure, and distinct profiles: this is where you will find a velvety reserve Merlot, a very drinkable and bright cuvée with floral aromatics, and an expressive and lively, full-bodied claret.

Winemaker Aryn Morell—a former chemical engineering student who started out in Napa by working in a lab for the Silver Oak winery—has been producing wines for Matthews since 2007.

He looks for balance and restraint with his wines, and to have the right amount of fruit to appeal to the average consumer. "Our wines are precise and classically made," he says. "You never feel like we'll punish you with our wines, even with a reserve claret, which has the highest tannin content."

With Aryn as head winemaker, Matthews' wines have changed very little over the years. Fans who enjoyed the wines a decade ago can still rely on Matthews

today to deliver consistency in quality and taste. "For us, there's an everlasting commitment to be as close to perfection as possible."

But Matthews prides itself on being more than just a winery: it's also about food, people, and community. With over eight acres of land in Woodinville, the property also contains a two-story bed-and-breakfast, an organic farm, and an outdoor kitchen. The on-site tasting room is also a notable venue for intimate dinners, corporate meetings, or large occasional gatherings, making it a great weekend destination to visit with friends. And with good wine, shared laughter, and panoramic views of the Sammamish Valley to boot, what's not to love?

DAIKON OYSTERS

with Soy Vinaigrette CHEF: SHOTA NAKAJIMA, ADANA

SERVES 2

SOY VINAIGRETTE
6 Tbsp mirin
¼ cup rice vinegar
1 tsp kosher salt
½ tsp soy sauce
Pinch of bonito flakes

DAIKON OYSTERS
¼ cup grated daikon radish
¼ cup Soy Vinaigrette (see here)
2 shiso leaves, cut into thin strips
½ tsp grated lime zest
8 Shigoku oysters, shucked
Soy-marinated ikura (see Note)

NOTE: Ikura is salmon caviar. Soy-marinated ikura can be found at Uwajimaya or any Japanese food store.

WINE PAIRING: Matthews Sauvignon Blanc

This dish plays off on a Japanese abalone dish and is served with an umami-rich soy vinaigrette. Matthews' Sauvignon Blanc comes from some of the highest-planted vineyards in the state, giving the wine enough acid and weight to cut through the brine of the oysters and marry well with the overall texture of the entire dish.

SOY VINAIGRETTE In a saucepan, combine mirin, vinegar, salt, and soy sauce and bring to a boil over high heat. Add bonito flakes and turn off heat. Set aside for 1 hour, then strain.

DAIKON OYSTERS In a bowl, combine daikon and soy vinaigrette. Mix in shiso and lime zest.

Arrange oysters on a bed of ice. Top oysters with daikon and garnish with ikura. Serve immediately.

SOY-MARINATED BLACK
COD with Kabocha CHEF: SHOTA NAKAJIMA, ADANA

SOY-MARINATED BLACK COD
2 (3-oz) black cod fillets, skin on
½ cup soy sauce
½ cup + 1 Tbsp mirin
½ cup sake

KABOCHA SQUASH PURÉE
¼ kabocha, deseeded and cut
　　into 1-inch cubes
2 cups dashi
3 Tbsp soy sauce
3 Tbsp mirin
7 oz firm tofu

ASSEMBLY
Soybean oil, for deep-frying
¼ kabocha, thinly sliced
1 quantity Kabocha Squash Purée
　　(see here)
Candied pecans, for garnish
　　(optional)
¼ kabocha, cubed (optional)

WINE PAIRING: Matthews Claret

The Matthews Winery's claret is one of those reliable go-to wines that work equally well for a special occasion or with a midweek meal. And it's versatile enough to complement an array of dishes, including chef Shota Nakajima's refined dish of soy-marinated black cod and rich kabocha squash purée.

While soy sauce is mostly enjoyed as a condiment, it can be used to enhance the flavor of a dish. Here, the fish is cured in a marinade of soy sauce, mirin, and sake and grilled to perfection. It's a simple but flavorful dish that suits a medium-bodied wine such as the claret. Pinot Noir will be jealous!

SOY-MARINATED BLACK COD In a bowl, combine cod skin-side up, soy sauce, mirin, and sake and set aside to marinate for 4 hours in the refrigerator.

KABOCHA SQUASH PURÉE In a saucepan, combine kabocha, dashi, soy sauce, and mirin and cook over medium-low heat for 20 minutes, until squash is tender. Transfer mixture and tofu into a blender and purée until smooth. Set aside.

ASSEMBLY Preheat broiler to high heat.

Remove black cod from marinade, then transfer to a baking sheet. Broil skin-side up for 10 minutes, until golden brown. Remove from the oven and set aside.

Heat oil in a deep fryer or deep saucepan to 300°F. Carefully lower sliced kabocha into the hot oil and deep-fry for 5 minutes, until golden. Transfer kabocha to a paper-towel-lined plate. (Alternatively, brush kabocha with oil and bake in a 250°F oven for 10 minutes, until golden brown.)

Place a dollop of purée onto the center of each plate. Arrange black cod on top, then garnish with deep-fried kabocha, candied pecans, or kabocha cubes, if using.

NEFARIOUS CELLARS

+

HEATHER AND DEAN NEFF

When Heather and Dean Neff (who put the "Nef" in Nefarious) first started dating in 1996, they bonded over their farming backgrounds and agricultural practices. His family owned an orchard in Wenatchee, and as luck would have it, her family owned the adjacent golf course in Pateros. (Heather was, literally, the girl next door.) They would often engage in starry-eyed conversations about their winemaking aspirations. And eventually, they took a leap of faith to live out their dream.

The couple moved to Oregon to learn more about enology and viticulture at Chemeketa Community College (well known for its wine studies), all the while working in wineries in the Willamette Valley. In 2004, they bought their Lake Chelan property and spent a year building their winemaking facility and planting the vineyards. On Valentine's Day in 2006 (to mark a winery born out of romance), Heather and Dean opened the tasting room.

As the sixth winery in the valley, Nefarious Cellars began with two grapes that thrive in Chelan—Viognier and Syrah—and later added Malbec. Dean's 2016 Nefarious Rx-3 is a spicy Rhône-style blend of Mourvèdre, Syrah, and Grenache, whereas Heather's delicate 2018 Viognier has apricot and grapefruit accents (which makes it a great accompaniment to barbecued seafood). "I pick white wine grapes with lower brix [sugar content] than most winemakers do, so they're not quite as high in alcohol," says Heather. "Our wines by nature are pretty wines because you get that with less alcohol." *Food & Wine* magazine hailed Nefarious as one of the best Washington wineries to visit, and their wines frequently win awards and recognition.

Even after all these years, the romance of winemaking is still intact. "The reality of owning a winery eventually sets in, but the love for the process never dies." And if you're keen to experience winery living, you might be tempted to visit their lofty guesthouse, which overlooks the estate's vineyard.

MAPO TOFU "SLOPPY JOE"

CHEF: JOSH HENDERSON, HUXLEY WALLACE COLLECTIVE

SERVES 6

QUICK PICKLES

½ cup plain white vinegar
½ cup rice vinegar
¼ cup granulated sugar
1 tsp kosher salt
2 carrots, cut into matchsticks
  (1 cup)
½ small daikon radish, cut into
  matchsticks (1 cup)

MAPO TOFU "SLOPPY JOE"

2 lbs ground pork
¾ cup pork or chicken stock,
  warmed
6 Tbsp soy sauce
2 Tbsp olive oil
½ cup yellow onion, finely
  chopped
2 cloves garlic, finely chopped
1 Tbsp grated ginger
6 Tbsp sake
1 Tbsp chili flakes
3 Tbsp yellow miso paste
1 Tbsp gochujang (Korean chili
  paste)
2 tsp instant dashi powder
2 tsp sesame oil
1 tsp Szechuan peppercorns,
  ground
1 tsp black pepper
½ tsp ground white pepper
Pinch of five-spice powder
5 oz medium-firm tofu, cut into
  ½-inch cubes

ASSEMBLY

Olive oil or butter, for toasting
6 seeded hamburger buns
3 cups Mapo Tofu "Sloppy Joe"
  (see here)
1 cup Quick Pickles (see here)
6 Tbsp Kewpie or regular
  mayonnaise

WINE PAIRING: Nefarious Defiance Vineyard Viognier

Josh Henderson's Huxley Wallace crew created this recipe for the Feast Portland Sandwich Invitational. His version takes inspiration from a classic Chinese dish and combines pork and tofu with a spicy, umami-laden seasoning.

Nefarious Cellars' Viognier is a crisp white wine with an expressive floral bouquet, which makes it a suitable counterpart for this aromatic dish.

QUICK PICKLES Combine vinegars, sugar, salt, and 1 cup water in a saucepan and cook over medium heat until sugar and salt have dissolved. Turn off heat.

In a large mason jar, combine carrots and radish. Pour pickling liquid into the jar and set aside to cool to room temperature. Refrigerate for at least 1 hour.

MAPO TOFU "SLOPPY JOE" In a large bowl, combine pork, stock, and soy sauce and break up chunks.

Heat oil in a large skillet over medium-high heat. Add onion, garlic, and ginger and sauté for 10 minutes, until onion is softened and browned on the edges. Pour in sake and cook for another 5 minutes, until reduced by half. Add pork and reduce heat to medium. Add chili flakes, miso, gochujang, dashi powder, sesame oil, and spices and cook for another 10 minutes, until pork is cooked through. (It should be similar to the consistency of chili. Break up any chunks, if necessary.)

Reduce heat to a simmer, then add tofu. Gently mix until tofu is well coated. Keep warm.

ASSEMBLY Heat oil (or butter) in a skillet over medium-high heat. Add buns flat-side down and lightly fry for 1 to 2 minutes, until toasted.

Transfer buns to a large serving plate. Scoop ½ cup of mapo tofu over the bottom bun. Top with quick pickles and a drizzle of mayonnaise. Top with the remaining half of the bun and serve immediately.

GIGANTE BEANS with Tomato Sauce
CHEF: JOSH HENDERSON, HUXLEY WALLACE COLLECTIVE

SERVES 10

WINE PAIRING: Nefarious Estate Syrah, Defiance Vineyard

In this easy comfort dish, created by chef Zoi Antonitsas while at Westward (formerly owned by Huxley Wallace), large gigante beans are slow-cooked in a rich tomato sauce and served with sliced baguette and feta. With a side of simple salad, it makes for a tasty and satisfying lunch.

With the aroma of bramble fruit and a smooth light taste, the Syrah by Nefarious Cellars makes a pleasing companion that will bring a smile to your face.

GIGANTE BEANS In a large bowl, soak beans in 3 quarts water overnight.

Preheat oven to 325°F.

Drain, then transfer beans to a large roasting pan or Dutch oven and add another 3 quarts of water. Bring to a simmer over high heat and cook for 30 minutes, skimming off any foam. Turn off heat, then add garlic, bay leaf, and chili flakes.

Cover with a lid, or parchment and aluminum foil, and bake for 1 hour. Stir beans and bake for another 30 minutes, until they are nearly cooked through.

TOMATO SAUCE Heat oil in a large saucepan over medium heat. Add onion, garlic, cinnamon, bay leaf, and salt and cook for 7 to 10 minutes, until onion is translucent but not caramelized. Add Syrah and cook for another 7 to 10 minutes, until reduced by half. Add tomato sauce (or tomatoes) and chili flakes and cook on low for 45 minutes.

From the pan of beans, drain out all but 2 cups of the cooking liquid. Add enough tomato sauce to the beans until mixture is saucy. Bake, uncovered, for another 30 minutes, until beans are tender and creamy but not falling apart. Season with salt, then set aside to cool. Refrigerate, uncovered, overnight. Reheat before serving.

ASSEMBLY Spoon beans into bowls. Garnish with feta, salt, and parsley, if using. Drizzle with oil and serve warm or room temperature with crusty baguette.

GIGANTE BEANS
4 cups dried gigante beans or white kidney beans
3 cloves garlic, finely chopped
1 bay leaf
Pinch of chili flakes

TOMATO SAUCE
2 Tbsp extra-virgin olive oil
1 yellow onion, chopped
1 clove garlic, thinly sliced
1 stick cinnamon
1 fresh bay leaf
1 tsp kosher salt
1 cup Syrah
4 cups tomato sauce or crushed tomatoes
1 tsp chili flakes
Salt, to taste

ASSEMBLY
Crumbled feta
Finishing salt
Parsley, for garnish (optional)
Good-quality olive oil
Crusty baguette, sliced

PEARL AND STONE WINE CO.

✚

PAUL RIBARY, CHRIS STONE, AND ROB WESORICK

Pearl and Stone might sound like an overt homage to the Pacific Northwest's natural mineral deposits, but the name is actually a combination of Chris Stone's surname and the first initials of co-owners Paul and Erika Ribary and Rob and Laurie Wesorick (PEARL; the A is for "and").

"We were three couples raising kids, and we often spoke of doing a wine project together," says Chris, who was already working at the Washington State Wine Commission.

"Basically," adds Rob, who works in project management, "Paul and I were living vicariously through Chris, who would taste wonderful wines and have these great experiences."

"One late evening, likely after a few glasses of wine, one of us suggested making some wine and just seeing what happens. Within half an hour, our LLC was registered,"

adds Paul, who owns a construction company and is, by default, the team's go-to equipment troubleshooter.

That was January 2013, when the popular wine style had massive flavor, high alcohol, and lots of new oak. "These days, we want more balanced wines with a little more acid and brighter fruit," says Chris. They choose not to filter their red wines, which allows the vineyard and the fruit to do most of the work.

Their Bordeaux-style blends are named after local mountains (think Resolution Peaks) and Rhône-style blends after local hiking trails (such as Boulder Loop).

Others such as Unemployment Beach and Old Rickety are named after local landmarks. A sense of wayfaring is the common thread in these names, which seems fitting for three friends whose thirst for a shared adventure inspired a new winery.

GRENACHE-STEAMED MUSSELS, Crispy Finocchiona, and Chimichurri Sauce CHEF: KRISTEN WATTS

SCHUMACHER, HEIRLOOM COOKSHOP

CHIMICHURRI SAUCE
4 cloves garlic
1 shallot, finely chopped
½ cup chopped cilantro
½ cup chopped parsley
½ cup chopped basil
1 tsp chili flakes
1 tsp kosher salt
½ cup red wine vinegar
1 cup olive oil

MUSSELS
2 lbs mussels, cleaned
½ lb finocchiona sausage, cut into thin disks
½ lb bacon or pancetta, finely chopped
1 large shallot, finely chopped
1 clove garlic, finely chopped
Pinch of chili flakes
1 cup red wine (preferably Grenache)

ASSEMBLY
½ cup chopped parsley, for garnish

WINE PAIRING: Pearl and Stone Boulder Loop Grenache

The Boulder Loop has a richness that can stand up to the big flavors and textures in this dish. A little heat in the chimichurri—along with the deliciously crispy sausage—pairs well with the wine.

CHIMICHURRI SAUCE Combine all ingredients except the oil in a food processor. Slowly drizzle in the oil as you pulse the ingredients.

MUSSELS Preheat oven to 375°F.

Discard any mussels that have cracked shells. Remove the beards and scrub them in cold water. Reserve in the refrigerator covered with ice until needed, but no longer than 3 hours.

Spread out the finocchiona on a baking sheet and bake for 30 minutes, until crispy.

In a large Dutch oven or deep skillet, add bacon (or pancetta) and brown over medium-low heat, until cooked through. Add shallot, garlic, and chili flakes and sauté for 5 minutes, until shallot is translucent.

Pour in wine and bring to a boil. Add mussels and bring the liquid to a simmer over medium-high heat. Cover and cook for 3 minutes, until mussels have just started to open. Discard any mussels that remain unopened.

ASSEMBLY In prepared bowls, ladle in the mussels and stock, top with chimichurri, and then sprinkle crispy sausage and parsley on top.

GREEN-GARLIC RISOTTO
with Seared Scallops and Maitake Mushrooms

CHEF: KRISTEN WATTS SCHUMACHER, HEIRLOOM COOKSHOP

Pictured p. 181

Pictured p. 181

SERVES 4

WINE PAIRING: Pearl and Stone Unemployment Beach Rosé

This spectacular risotto tastes as good as it looks. Chef Kristen Watts Schumacher encourages readers to take the time to cook the mushrooms until they turn crispy as it adds such an incredibly textural contrast to the risotto and scallops.

A beautiful dry rosé pairs nicely with rich yet vibrant dishes, and Pearl and Stone's Unemployment Beach Rosé has a clean and crisp taste and finish that complements a creamy risotto—it's the perfect summer romance.

RISOTTO Separate the bulb of the green garlic from the stalk. Rinse well, then finely chop the bulb and roughly chop the stalks.

Bring stock to a boil in a large saucepan. Add the green garlic stalks and cook for 2½ minutes, until tender. Add arugula and cook for another 30 seconds. Using a slotted spoon, transfer stalks and arugula to a bowl of ice water. Reserve the stock.

Transfer the green garlic stalks and arugula to a food processor and process until smooth. Add cold water, a teaspoon at a time, until it has an even consistency. Season with salt.

Heat oil and 2 tablespoons butter in a medium saucepan over medium heat. Add the green garlic bulb and shallot, season with salt, and sauté for 8 to 10 minutes, until tender. Add rice, season with more salt, and stir for 2 to 3 minutes, until rice is fragrant and nutty.

RISOTTO

2 green garlic (spring garlic or young garlic)
6 cups chicken stock
2 cups packed arugula
Kosher salt, to taste
2 Tbsp olive oil
½ cup (1 stick) butter (divided)
1 large shallot, chopped
1 cup arborio rice
½ cup dry unoaked white wine
½ cup grated Parmesan or Grana Padano
Black pepper, to taste

SEARED SCALLOPS AND MAITAKE MUSHROOMS

½ cup + 2 Tbsp (1¼ sticks) cold butter, cut into pieces (divided)

2 lbs maitake mushrooms, trimmed and finely chopped

Kosher salt and black pepper, to taste

1 Tbsp olive oil

12 large sea scallops

½ cup white wine

Juice of 1 lemon

¼ cup soy sauce

ASSEMBLY

¼ cup finely chopped parsley, for garnish

Pour in wine and simmer for 5 to 8 minutes, stirring constantly, until the liquid is absorbed. Add ½ cup of stock and stir for 10 minutes, until stock is absorbed. Repeat until almost all of the stock is used and rice is al dente but not undercooked. If needed, add a little more stock to create a loose, fluid texture known as *all'onda*, which means wavy or "creating waves." Stir in the remaining 6 tablespoons butter. Remove from heat and stir in Parmesan (or Grana Padano). Season with salt and pepper.

Swirl in all but 2 tablespoons of green garlic purée: just enough to incorporate, but still bright and streaky. Keep warm.

SEARED SCALLOPS AND MAITAKE MUSHROOMS Melt ¼ cup (½ stick) butter in large skillet over medium-high heat. Add mushrooms and sauté for 12 minutes, until golden brown and crispy. Season with salt and pepper. Remove from heat.

Heat oil in the same skillet over high heat. Sprinkle scallops with salt and pepper and add them to the pan. Cook for 2 minutes on each side, until just opaque in center. Transfer scallops to a plate and set aside.

In the same pan, combine wine, lemon juice, and soy sauce and boil for 2 minutes, scraping the caramelized bits off the bottom of the pan. Reduce heat to low. Add the remaining 6 tablespoons butter, a piece at a time, whisking until melted and smooth. Season with salt and pepper.

ASSEMBLY Mound risotto on each plate and gently arrange three large scallops on top. Sprinkle with crispy mushrooms and drizzle with more green garlic purée and chopped parsley.

SEVEN HILLS WINERY

+

CASEY McCLELLAN

Winemaker Casey McClellan's agricultural roots run deep in eastern Washington. He's a fourth-generation farmer, whose family has lived in eastern Washington since the late nineteenth century. In the early 1980s, Casey and his father planted twenty-one acres of vineyards in what is known today as the founding blocks of Seven Hills Winery. Unbeknownst to Casey at the time, these grounds would eventually become the appellation's oldest commercial plantings of Cabernet Sauvignon and Merlot—the winery's most popular varietals from a single vineyard site—and emerge as one of the Pacific Northwest's sites for *grand cru* (the finest of wines).

"We have a great love of Cabernet Sauvignon, Merlot, and Bordeaux red varietals in general, so we focus on those," says Casey. "We're blessed to live in a region that can grow almost anything."

Seven Hills Winery is the fifth registered winery in Walla Walla, behind Waterbrook, L'Ecole N° 41 (page 146), Woodward Canyon, and Leonetti. In an industry that values longevity and tradition, Casey is one of the longest continuous winemakers in Washington state, which is something to toast.

HAMACHI CRUDO with

Avocado Mousse CHEF: SHAUN MCCRAIN, COPINE

CRUDO TOPPINGS

2 oz dried shiitake mushrooms
½ cup + 2 Tbsp granulated sugar
　(divided)
1 cup rice vinegar
1 ruby red grapefruit, segmented
　and cut into small bite-sized
　pieces
1 Fresno chile, deseeded,
　deveined, and thinly sliced
1 French Breakfast radish, thinly
　sliced with a mandoline

AVOCADO MOUSSE

1 Hass avocado
2 Tbsp olive oil
1 Tbsp lime juice
Salt, to taste

ASSEMBLY

Grated zest and juice of 1 lime
1 Tbsp coarse or flaky sea salt
½ lb sashimi-grade hamachi
Extra-virgin olive oil, for drizzling
Micro radish sprouts, for garnish

WINE PAIRING: Seven Hills Winery Sauvignon Blanc

Crudo, the Italian word for "raw," often signals a dish that is pure, minimally handled, and naturally delicious. This hamachi crudo—with shiitakes, French Breakfast radishes, and Fresno chiles—speaks to the flavors of the Pacific Northwest. Just be sure to use sashimi-grade hamachi for quality, and keep the fish chilled until you're ready to slice and plate.

Seven Hills' Sauvignon Blanc has a lavish bouquet of herb, pineapple, pink grapefruit, licorice, and clove aromas. The tart acidity highlights the crispness and acidity of the crudo's components and cuts through the creamy avocado mousse.

CRUDO TOPPINGS In a large bowl, submerge shiitake mushrooms in 4 cups boiling water and set aside for 30 minutes. Drain mushrooms, reserving ½ cup of the water. (Remaining water can be used for stock or sauce.)

Cut mushrooms into ¼-inch slices, then add them to a large saucepan. Add ½ cup sugar, vinegar, and reserved mushroom water and cook over high heat for 5 to 10 minutes, until liquid is reduced by half. Drain mushrooms, slice, and reserve for plating.

In a small bowl, combine grapefruit and the remaining 2 tablespoons sugar. Set aside for 10 minutes. (This helps to sweeten the grapefruit, firm it up, and remove some of the harsh acidity.)

Place chile and radish in separate bowls of ice water until needed.

AVOCADO MOUSSE In a blender, combine all ingredients and blend until smooth. Store in a piping bag until needed.

ASSEMBLY Using a mortar and pestle, combine lime zest and salt.

Slice hamachi as thinly as possible, then arrange on four plates. Lightly drizzle oil on hamachi and add a little lime juice and lime salt. Arrange sliced shiitake, grapefruit, chile, and radish on top. Finish with a piping of avocado mousse and garnish with radish sprouts. Serve immediately.

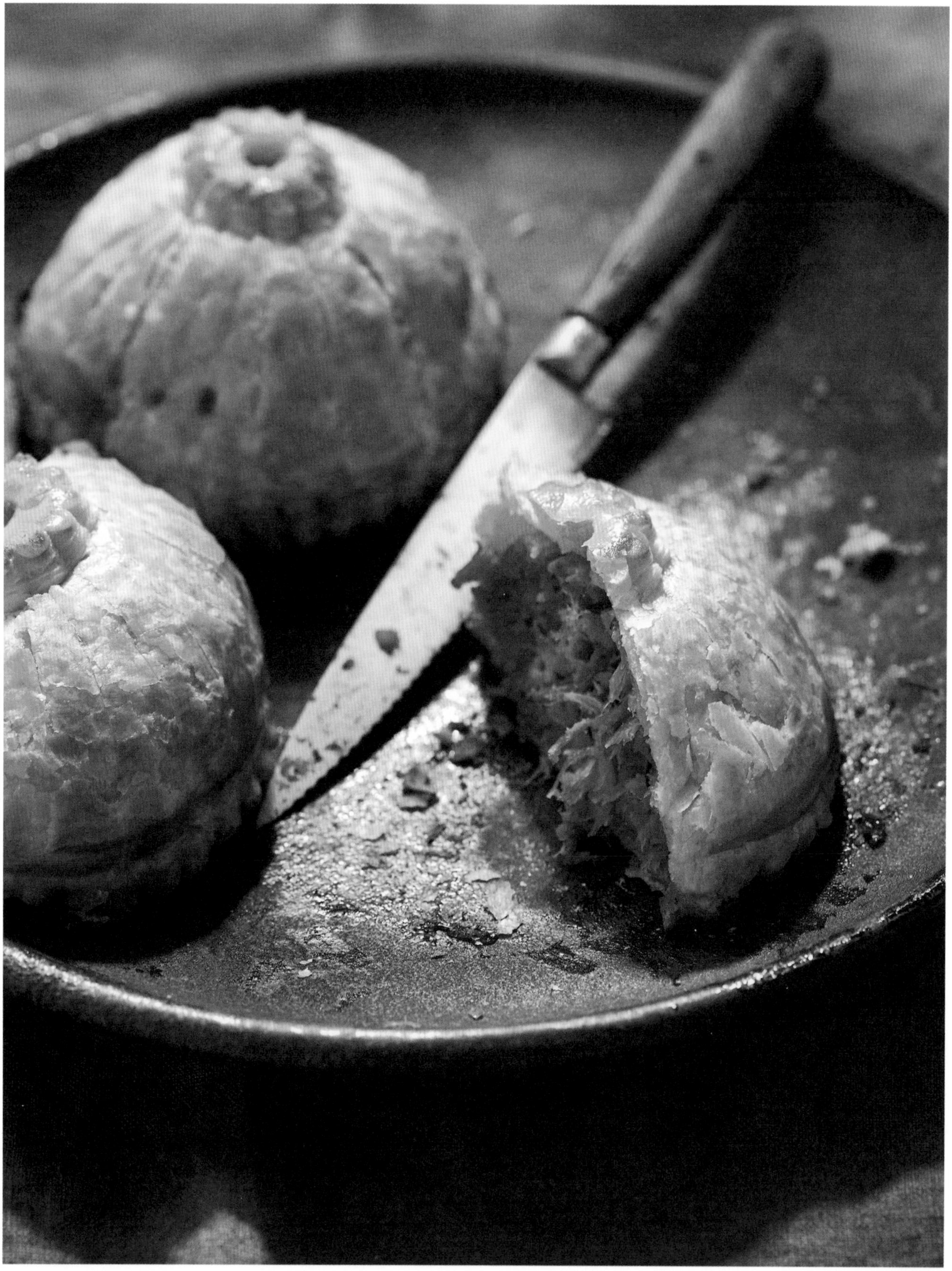

Duck-Confit Pithiviers | *p. 188*

DUCK-CONFIT
PITHIVIERS CHEF: SHAUN MCCRAIN, COPINE

Pictured p. 187

SERVES 2

WINE PAIRING: Seven Hills Winery Seven Hills Vineyard Merlot

This classic French pastry is a signature dish at Copine. Chef Shaun McCrain replaces the laborious handmade dough that is used at the restaurant with good-quality store-bought dough. Just be sure to set aside a few hours to chill the duck legs.

Here, it's paired with Seven Hills Winery's intriguing single-vineyard Merlot with wispy aromas of green pepper, spice, and raspberry. The wine has juicy fruit that highlights the subtle orange flavor as well as the earthiness of the duck.

DUCK-CONFIT PITHIVIERS Remove duck legs and place them on a baking sheet or large plate and season generously with salt. Chill for 3 hours, uncovered.

Meanwhile, remove the breasts and take off skin and fat. Chop the skin and fat and place in a saucepan set over low heat and slowly cook for 30 minutes, until the fat is rendered. This mixture will be used to confit the legs. Reserve breasts.

Preheat oven to 225°F.

Rinse legs under cold running water. Arrange them in a small but deep baking dish and pour the rendered fat over the duck. (The legs should be completely submerged.) Put in the oven and simmer for 2 to 3 hours, until the duck is tender and meat can be easily pulled off the bone. Set aside to cool.

In a saucepan, combine onion, honey, and vinegar and cook for 15 minutes over medium heat, until it has reduced by half. Add stock and cook for another 20 to 25 minutes, until it has reduced to a thick sauce. Set aside.

When duck is cool enough to handle, pick meat off the bone and put it in a bowl. Pour in duck sauce and mix well.

DUCK-CONFIT PITHIVIERS
1 (5-lb) whole duck
Kosher salt
½ white onion, chopped
½ cup honey
½ cup red wine vinegar
2 cups beef stock
2 eggs (divided)
1 egg yolk
Grated zest and juice of 1 large orange
1 (17-oz) package good-quality puff pastry dough, thawed

1 cup torn frisée
2 finely chopped chives
3 sprigs parsley
1 tsp extra-virgin olive oil
Squeeze of lemon juice
Salt and black pepper, to taste

In a food processor, combine duck breasts with one egg and the extra yolk and purée until smooth. Add this mousse to the confit mixture, then stir in orange zest and juice and mix well. Divide mixture in half and shape into two balls, flattening the bottom. Chill for about 2 hours, until firm. Measure the diameter of the ball, and use a ring mold one inch larger than the diameter of the balls.

Roll out puff pastry dough to a ¼-inch thickness. Using a ring mold, cut out four disks one inch larger than the diameter of the balls. Reserve the pastry trim.

Place remaining egg in a small bowl, add a few drops of water, and mix thoroughly. Place each ball in the center of a disk. Lightly brush the exposed edges with egg wash, then cover each ball with another pastry disk, stretching the edges gently over the ball. Using the ring mold, press edges together to trim and seal. Using a small ring mold, cut out a circle from the pastry trim to create a decorative topper for each pithivier. Gently brush egg wash over the entire pithivier, and using a small pastry tip, create a hole at the top of the dome for venting. Chill in refrigerator for 15 minutes.

Preheat oven to 350°F.

Place pastries on a baking sheet and bake for 20 to 30 minutes, until puffed and golden. Remove pastry from oven and using a serrated knife, slice in half.

ASSEMBLY In a bowl, combine frisée, chives, and parsley.

In a separate bowl, combine oil and lemon juice. Dress salad, then season to taste with salt and pepper.

Place the pithivier on a serving plate and serve immediately with herb salad.

SIGHTGLASS CELLARS

+

SEAN BOYD

Sean Boyd was destined for wine-making—he just didn't realize it until he was a young adult. You see, his father, Gerald, was a well-regarded editor of *Wine Spectator* in the early 1980s and a veteran wine writer for the *San Francisco Chronicle*.

At the age of twenty, Sean traveled to Australia and took a job as a cellar worker at one of the country's oldest wineries, Penfolds. "I had never worked so hard in my life," Sean says. "For the first two weeks, I thought it was terrible." And then the light bulb switched on, and the work no longer felt arduous. "Every day was unique, and I loved the crafting of the wines." Sean helped Penfolds through a single harvest, and then traveled around the world and took on work stints at various wineries, including Rosemount Estate in Australia, Torres in Spain, and Ramos Pinto in Portugal.

He eventually put his wine knowledge to work when he moved to Seattle in the late 1990s and began making wine at Woodinville Wine Cellars, where he stayed on for fourteen years until it closed. In 2016, he started production on his own wines, using the facilities at JM Cellars, and launched Sightglass Cellars. (A sight glass is used to observe the clarity of wine.) Two years later, Sean and his wife, Kristin, moved into their own facility.

Sean, who is a massive advocate of Washington Cabernet Franc, is also known for his Cabernet Sauvignon. His style is a combination of Old and New World wines, with a lean toward the latter.

"My philosophy is to allow the grapes to speak for themselves," he explains. The result? Wines that are lighter on the oak, tart, and crisp. "My wines today are a continuation of my work at Woodinville Wine Cellars."

And in case there was any doubt, Gerald is a fan of Sean's wine. "My dad is, of course, proud of my success in the business and has even provided positive feedback to the wines!" To quote an old adage, the bunch doesn't fall far from the vine.

GRILLED QUAIL
with Guanciale and Oyster Mushrooms

CHEF: DAVID NICHOLS, EIGHT ROW

4 semiboneless quail
¼ cup olive oil (divided)
2 tsp kosher salt, plus extra
    to taste
2 tsp black pepper, plus extra
    to taste
½ lb guanciale or good-quality
    unsmoked bacon, cubed
    (1½ cups)
2 cups oyster mushrooms
1 shallot, sliced
2 cloves garlic, sliced
2 Tbsp sherry vinegar
¼ cup red wine
1 cup cherry tomatoes, halved
2 tsp chopped thyme
1½ cups veal stock
2 Tbsp butter
2 Tbsp chopped parsley
1 cup frisée, for garnish (optional)

WINE PAIRING: Sightglass Cabernet Franc

Chef David Nichols loves to prepare this dish in the spring: smoky grilled quail pairs wonderfully with the sherry vinegar, but the fresh tomatoes add an undeniable brightness. The rich and well-balanced Cabernet Franc, with aromas of fresh herbs, coffee, and char, will stand up to the grilled quail and the dish's subtle acidity from the tomatoes and vinegar.

Preheat grill to medium heat.

Brush quail with 2 tablespoons oil, then season with 2 teaspoons each of salt and pepper. Place quail on the grill and cook for 7 minutes on each side, until the quail can be easily released from the grill. Transfer to a platter and set aside.

Meanwhile, heat remaining 2 tablespoons oil in a large skillet over medium heat. Add guanciale (or bacon) and sauté for 6 minutes, until browned. Transfer guanciale to a paper-towel-lined plate.

Heat the reserved oil in the pan over high heat. Add mushrooms, season with salt and pepper, and cook for 2 minutes. Add shallot and garlic and cook for another 2 minutes, until mushrooms are cooked through.

Pour in vinegar and wine and simmer for 4 to 5 minutes, until reduced by half. Add tomatoes and thyme and stir. Pour in stock, reduce heat to medium, and cook for 6 minutes, until sauce is thick enough to coat the back of a spoon. Remove from heat and stir in butter and parsley, until the butter has melted. Season with salt and pepper to taste.

Transfer three-quarters of the sauce, guanciale, and mushrooms to a rimmed serving platter. Arrange quail on top and add the remaining sauce. Garnish with frisée, if using.

CRAB TOAST with Shaved Apple and Fennel Chimichurri CHEF: DAVID NICHOLS, EIGHT ROW

SERVES 4

FENNEL CHIMICHURRI

2 Tbsp chopped fennel fronds
1 Tbsp chopped parsley
1 Tbsp chopped chives
1 Tbsp finely chopped shallot
1 tsp kosher salt
1 tsp black pepper
½ tsp fennel seeds, toasted
½ tsp chili flakes
1½ Tbsp olive oil
1½ Tbsp lemon juice
1 Tbsp orange juice

CRAB TOAST

1 Tbsp extra-virgin olive oil
4 slices sourdough bread
4 cloves garlic
1 lb Dungeness crabmeat, picked clean of shells
1 bulb fennel, cut into matchsticks (1 cup)
1 Granny Smith apple, cut into matchsticks
1 Tbsp lemon juice
¼ cup Fennel Chimichurri (see here)
2 tsp kosher salt
2 tsp black pepper
½ cup fennel fronds, chopped

WINE PAIRING: Sightglass Chardonnay

The next time you host a party, regale your guests with a dish that's sure to impress and that's worthy of social-media posts. You can prepare much of it in advance so that minimal prep work is needed when guests start to arrive.

This dish is best served on a warm day with a glass of chilled Sightglass Chardonnay. With crisp citrus notes, it makes for a lovely and gentle accompaniment that accentuates the sweetness of the crab and amplifies the freshness of the chimichurri.

FENNEL CHIMICHURRI In a bowl, combine all ingredients and mix well.

CRAB TOAST Preheat oven to 400°F.

Brush oil on one side of bread, place on a baking sheet, and toast for 2 minutes on each side, until golden brown. Rub garlic on one side of the toasted bread.

In a bowl, combine crabmeat, fennel, apple, lemon juice, chimichurri, salt, and pepper and fold. Top the toast with the crab mixture and garnish with fennel fronds. Serve.

SLEIGHT OF HAND CELLARS

+

TREY BUSCH

If you're a Pearl Jam fan, Sleight of Hand is likely a familiar name.

The song happens to be one of Trey Busch's favorites and speaks to his journey from corporate America to winemaking. In fact, it was Seattle's grunge scene that inspired Trey to move here from Atlanta in the early 1990s.

Feeling uninspired by his office job at the time, Trey moved to Walla Walla in 2000 at the urging of fellow winemaker (and former record-store owner) Jamie Brown and worked for the late Eric Dunham at Dunham Cellars. Two years later, Trey moved onto Basel Cellars and eventually launched his own wine label with his friends and business partners Jerry and Sandy Solomon.

Sleight of Hand Cellars specializes in Bordeaux blends, but Trey especially loves making Syrah. His 2015 Levitation Syrah earned a spot on *Wine Spectator*'s Top 100

list. For those who are new to his wines, the Magician Riesling is a good starting point. "It has a tiny amount of residual sugar to balance out the racy acidity, and it's great for novices and experts alike."

Trey doesn't look to produce the biggest, ripest, and oakiest wines—especially with the Bordeaux varieties. "We try to make more elegant wines that still show a ton of fruit, but hopefully that fruit reflects its terroir." It may be one reason why wine critic Jeb Dunnuck named Sleight of Hand as one of Washington's top wineries in 2019.

But Trey hasn't forgotten his muse. Sleight of Hand, along with their friend Mark Ryan McNeilly of Mark Ryan Winery (page 160), collaborated to make a wine that benefitted the Vitalogy Foundation, the giving arm of Pearl Jam. "It was a way for us to stay attached to the band we love, but more importantly, it's a way for our dollars to go to something we care about."

And if you're into music as much as you are into wine, Sleight of Hand's tasting room is unlikely to be anything you've experienced before. Trey has accumulated a collection of three thousand vinyl records (and counting), which are on full display.

BEEF TARTARE with Anchovy and Garlic

CHEF: ETHAN STOWELL, ETHAN STOWELL RESTAURANTS

PRESERVED GARLIC

1 lemon
1 head garlic, peeled (12 to 15 cloves)
3 sprigs thyme
1 cup extra-virgin olive oil

BEEF TARTARE

1 (12-oz) New York strip or tenderloin, trimmed of excess fat and sinew
3 cloves Preserved Garlic (see here), smashed and finely chopped
4 anchovy fillets, finely chopped
Grated zest of ½ lemon
3 Tbsp extra-virgin olive oil
Kosher salt and black pepper, to taste
Parsley or sorrel, chopped, for garnish
Your favorite bread or crackers, to serve

WINE PAIRING: Sleight of Hand The Enchantress Chardonnay

A quality beef tartare requires minimal fussing, and Ethan Stowell's version relies on the simplicity of quality ingredients to speak volumes.

The racy acidity of this Chardonnay makes the perfect counterpoint for a rich beef tartare, while the underlying spice notes create a playful complexity with the zing of garlic and salty brine of anchovy.

PRESERVED GARLIC Using a vegetable peeler, peel three or four long strips of lemon zest. In a saucepan, combine zest, garlic, thyme, and oil. Simmer gently over low heat for 20 to 25 minutes, until garlic can be easily pierced with the tip of a knife. Pour into a glass jar with a lid and set aside. (Leftover preserved garlic can be refrigerated for up to 2 weeks.)

BEEF TARTARE Wrap the meat tightly in plastic wrap and freeze overnight.

In a large bowl, combine garlic and anchovies. Stir in lemon zest. Add oil and mix well.

Remove the meat from the freezer and unwrap. Using your sharpest knife, slice the meat into ¼-inch-thick slices, then crosscut the slices into ¼-inch strips. Cut across the strips to form a fine dice.

Add meat and 1 tablespoon water to the garlic mixture and toss gently. Season with salt and pepper to taste, garnish with parsley (or sorrel), and serve with bread (or crackers).

Potato Gnocchi with Beef Cheek Ragù | p. 198

POTATO GNOCCHI
with Beef Cheek Ragù

CHEF: ETHAN STOWELL, ETHAN STOWELL RESTAURANTS

Pictured p. 196

SERVES 4

WINE PAIRING: Sleight of Hand The Conjurer Red Blend

Known for his handmade pastas and crave-worthy sauces, chef and restaurateur Ethan Stowell always looks for elegance and finesse when matching red wine with a meaty dish. The Conjurer has that gentle hand with just enough smoky black fruit to play off a rich ragù and enough acid to stay light on the palate and give a clean finish.

BEEF CHEEK RAGÙ Heat oil in a Dutch oven over high heat. Add beef, reduce heat to medium-high, and brown for 8 to 10 minutes, breaking up lumps. Add carrot, onion, celery, and garlic and cook for 7 minutes, until vegetables are tender. Pour in wine and stir, scraping the caramelized bits off the bottom of the pan.

Meanwhile, put tomatoes in a food processor and purée. Strain out seeds. Add purée to pan and bring to a boil. Add bay leaves.

Reduce heat to low and simmer, uncovered, for 1½ to 2 hours, until the meat is very tender and sauce has thickened. Stir occasionally to prevent sticking. (If the liquid has evaporated before the meat is cooked through, add a little water and stir.) Remove the bay leaves and add oregano.

BEEF CHEEK RAGÙ
- 2 Tbsp extra-virgin olive oil
- 1½ lbs ground beef cheeks
- 1 carrot, finely diced (1 cup)
- 1 onion, finely diced (1 cup)
- 2 to 3 stalks celery, finely diced (1 cup)
- 4 cloves garlic, thinly sliced
- 1 cup white wine
- 2 (28-oz) cans San Marzano tomatoes, puréed
- 2 fresh bay leaves
- 2 Tbsp chopped oregano

2 large russet potatoes, unpeeled
    and scrubbed
Olive oil, for rubbing
Kosher salt
2 egg yolks, room temperature
½ cup "00" flour, plus extra for
    dusting

ASSEMBLY

Salt and black pepper, to taste
Grated Parmesan, for sprinkling

POTATO GNOCCHI Preheat oven to 350°F.

Place potatoes on a baking sheet and rub them in oil. Season with salt, then bake for 1 hour, until tender. Set aside to cool.

Line a baking sheet with parchment paper. Put potatoes through a ricer, letting them fall onto the parchment. (Alternatively, peel and mash potatoes by hand, making sure they are super tender.) Discard the skins. Spread potatoes out on the parchment and set aside to cool down until room temperature. Transfer potatoes to a bowl.

Add egg yolks and stir to combine. Sprinkle flour over the top and gently knead in the bowl until mixed through. Turn dough onto a lightly dusted board and knead until dough is no longer tacky. (If needed, add more flour.)

Divide dough into quarters. Roll each quarter into a log about ½ inch in diameter, and then cut into 1-inch pieces. Invert a fork so that the tines point down. Starting at the tines nearest the handle, roll the gnocchi firmly but gently down the tines, creating a slight curve and ridges as you go. Allow gnocchi to fall off the ends of the tines and onto a floured baking sheet. Set aside.

ASSEMBLY Bring a large saucepan of salted water to a boil. Gently lower gnocchi, in batches of 15 to 20, and cook for 1 to 2 minutes, until they float to the surface. Transfer to an oiled baking sheet and cover with thick plastic wrap. Repeat with the remaining batches.

Combine gnocchi and ragù and season with salt and pepper to taste. Place in bowls or a large serving platter and sprinkle Parmesan on top. Serve.

STRUCTURE CELLARS

+

BRIAN GRASSO AND BRANDEE SLOSAR

If anything is to rip a couple apart, turning a home into a winery probably ranks at the top. But instead, Brandee Slosar and Brian Grasso are thriving, years after Brian converted the couple's basement into a winemaking facility. In fact, the two had made more than 1,300 cases of wine in their home before securing their own tasting and production space in SODO Wine Works in 2013.

Brandee loves Cab Franc; Brian enjoys Syrah. While Brandee had been voraciously learning about wine since she was nineteen, Brian's love was instant. "He just came home one day and said he wanted to be a winemaker." After enrolling in the Northwest Wine Academy, Brian became a cellar worker at Darby and Baer wineries and took an internship at Sparkman, where he began making his own wine. In 2011, the couple became licensed winemakers and began making wine out of their Ballard home.

"Our wines are fruit forward," says Brian. "And we tend to make them in the least intrusive way. We employ some modern methods, but for the most part, our approach is pretty hands off."

Brandee's love of architecture, which she studied in college, was the inspiration behind the name. *Structure* also lends itself to the fact that Brian and Brandee were in the throes of a challenging home remodel/winery buildout when they started making wine. Popping open a bottle of Syrah—from the very first barrel they made in 2008—helped them get through it. "Brian picked up this Big Gulp cup and dumped the bottle into it and handed it to me, and just listened to me vent." Afterwards, Brian reminded Brandee that the house, like their wine, had good structure that just needed some time and love.

DUCK LIVER PÂTÉ with Pickled Huckleberries

CHEF: KYLE PETERSON, PALACE KITCHEN

PICKLED HUCKLEBERRIES
½ cup champagne vinegar
½ cup honey
½ lb huckleberries

DUCK LIVER PÂTÉ
1 lb duck livers, trimmed of sinew
  or stringy pieces
Salt
¼ cup canola oil (divided)
1 large shallot, chopped (¼ cup)
1½ fl oz rye whiskey or cognac
2 Tbsp apple cider vinegar, plus
  extra to taste
1½ cups (3 sticks) cold butter,
  cubed

ASSEMBLY
Crostini or crackers, to serve
Shaved radish, for garnish
Baby mustard greens, for garnish

WINE PAIRING: Structure "Triomphe" Mourvèdre

If you happen to be one of those people who are unconvinced by liver, this simple recipe may change your mind—a tasty duck liver pâté that can be whipped up in next to no time and served with baguette or crackers for an easy appetizer. It keeps well in the refrigerator, which allows for advance preparation when desired. Chef Kyle Peterson recommends submerging the livers in milk or ice water for a few hours prior to cooking to remove some of the liver's bitterness.

It's appropriately paired with Structure Cellars' "Triomphe" Mourvèdre, which has plenty of deep fruit notes to pair well with duck liver and the acidity of the huckleberries.

PICKLED HUCKLEBERRIES In a saucepan, combine vinegar and honey and bring to a boil and cook until honey is dissolved. Put huckleberries in a bowl, pour in the mixture, and set aside, uncovered, for 1 hour in the refrigerator.

DUCK LIVER PÂTÉ Pat-dry duck livers with paper towels and season with salt. Set aside.

Heat 2 tablespoons oil in a skillet over medium-high heat. Add shallot and sauté for 4 minutes, until cooked through and translucent. Transfer mixture to a plate.

Heat remaining 2 tablespoons of oil in the same skillet over medium heat. Add liver and cook for 5 minutes, until still a little pink in the center. Pour in whiskey (or cognac) and cook for about a minute, until the flame dies.

Transfer liver and shallot to a high-speed blender, then add vinegar and purée.

Add butter a cube at a time, until the liver turns to a smooth paste. Season to taste with salt and more vinegar. Set aside, covered, or transfer to a piping bag to avoid oxidation.

ASSEMBLY Spread pâté on crostini (or crackers). Garnish with pickled huckleberries, radish, and mustard greens.

BRAISED RABBIT with
Einkorn Porridge and Morel Mushrooms

CHEF: KYLE PETERSON, PALACE KITCHEN

Pictured p. 203

SERVES 4 TO 6

WINE PAIRING: Structure "Foundation" Cabernet Franc

For this recipe, lean, mildly flavored rabbit is slow-cooked in a savory herb stock and paired with einkorn and earthy morel mushrooms. Einkorn, one of the oldest-known cultivated wheats, is not something commonly seen on menus, but this toothsome whole grain is delicious. Chef Kyle Peterson loves using morels for their versatility and the fact that they have a short spring harvest cycle, but any mushroom will work.

Cabernet Franc boasts dark fruit and herb notes that can stand up to the rich porridge and meaty mushrooms.

BRAISED RABBIT In a stockpot, combine salt, sugar, pepper, chili flakes, cloves, bay leaf, cinnamon, and 4 quarts water and bring to a boil. Remove from heat and set aside to cool. Submerge rabbit in the brine, then refrigerate overnight.

Preheat oven to 300°F.

Rinse rabbit under cold running water. Combine rabbit and stock in a roasting pan, cover with aluminum foil, and cook for 2½ hours, until fork tender. Set aside to cool, then pick meat off the bones and reserve.

PICKLED PEARL ONIONS In a bowl, combine onion rings and salt and set aside for 30 minutes.

Place the mustard seeds in a small saucepan, cover with cold water, and bring to a boil. Drain mustard seeds and repeat this process twice more.

Rinse onion rings under cool running water and put into a bowl. Add mustard seeds.

In small saucepan, combine vinegar, sugar, and ½ cup water and bring to a boil. Pour the hot pickling liquid over onions. Set aside to cool and refrigerate until needed.

BRAISED RABBIT
½ cup kosher salt
½ cup granulated sugar
1 Tbsp black pepper
1 tsp chili flakes
3 whole cloves
1 bay leaf
1 cinnamon stick
1 (3-lb) whole rabbit
2 quarts chicken stock

PICKLED PEARL ONIONS
1 cup pearl onions, cut into rings
2 tsp kosher salt
¼ cup mustard seeds
1 cup red wine vinegar
¾ cup granulated sugar

EINKORN PORRIDGE

2 cups einkorn or wheat berries
2 Tbsp canola oil
1 large shallot, finely chopped
    (¼ cup)
¼ cup thinly sliced green garlic
    (spring garlic or young garlic)
½ cup white wine
2½ quarts chicken stock
½ cup thinly sliced chives
¼ cup grated pecorino, for
    garnish
Salt, to taste
Lemon juice, to taste

MOREL MUSHROOMS

1 cup (2 sticks) butter
2 cloves garlic
2 sprigs thyme
2 sprigs rosemary
3 cups morel mushrooms,
    cleaned
Salt, to taste
Lemon juice, to taste

ASSEMBLY

Shaved pecorino, for garnish
Baby arugula, for garnish

EINKORN PORRIDGE Put einkorn (or wheat) in food processor and pulse until cracked.

Heat oil in large saucepan over high heat and toast einkorn for 2 minutes. Reduce heat to medium, add shallot and green garlic, and cook for 3 minutes, until both are translucent. Pour in wine and cook for 3 minutes, until evaporated. Add stock, reduce heat to medium-low, and simmer for 30 minutes, until einkorn is tender. Stir.

Remove from heat, then add chives and pecorino. Season with salt and lemon juice.

MOREL MUSHROOMS In small saucepan set over low heat, combine butter, garlic, and herbs and cook for 5 minutes. Add mushrooms and simmer for 5 minutes, until softened. Remove from heat and season with salt and lemon.

ASSEMBLY Spoon porridge into each bowl. Top with braised rabbit and mushrooms. Garnish with pickled onions, pecorino, and arugula. Serve immediately.

TWO MOUNTAIN WINERY

+

MATT RAWN

Matt Rawn was slightly more sophisticated than your average teenager. When he was fifteen, his uncle first introduced Matt to Leonetti, L'Ecole N° 41 (page 146), and Woodward Canyon wines. Despite the fact that he was drinking from a Solo cup, he enjoyed the flavor immediately.

In 2006, he and his brother, Patrick, took over the family-owned winery in Zillah. Situated in the Rattlesnake Hills within Yakima Valley, Two Mountain is renowned for its Hidden Horse Red Blend, Cabernet Franc, Riesling, and Lemberger. "But if I had to choose just one, it would be the Cab Franc," says Matt. "It grows really well in this area, and I think that people can taste the varietal characteristics clearly. And it tends to be one of our favorites."

Yakima Valley's warm days and cool nights provide the ideal growing conditions for grapes "to fully express their classic characteristics," and the Cascade mountain range offers a wonderful rain-shadow effect on the vineyards.

Matt credits his brother for helping to shape the personality of their wines. "Patrick is a fantastic grape grower," says Matt. "Our approach to winemaking is simple: we let the grapes do all the talking and stay out of the way. We let Washington be Washington. We let Zillah be Zillah."

Having grown up in Wenatchee, the brothers style their wines after the juice they were exposed to early on, finding inspiration in quintessential Washington wines that helped to forge their own paths in the industry. Matt shares, "At times, wines are analyzed in very formal settings, but other times, they need to be fun. You might find yourself perched on the tailgate of a pickup and drinking it out of a plastic cup because that's what you have available."

BRAISED PORK SHOULDER
with Fennel, Sage, and Hazelnuts

CHEF: JOSH HENDERSON, HUXLEY WALLACE COLLECTIVE

SERVES 6 TO 8

1 (3½-lb) boneless pork
   shoulder or butt
1 Tbsp olive oil
5 Tbsp cold butter (divided)
Salt and black pepper, to taste
3 shallots, thinly sliced
2 bulbs fennel, cored and sliced
   lengthwise into ½-inch-thick
   pieces
7 sage leaves, plus extra for
   garnish
1 cup Merlot
3 bay leaves
4 cups homemade pork, beef,
   or chicken stock
½ cup blanched hazelnuts
Finishing salt, for sprinkling

WINE PAIRING: Two Mountain Merlot

This rich and aromatic dish promises complexity and comfort all at the same time. And I encourage you to pair it with Two Mountain's Merlot. It has balanced notes of oak, cherry, and vanilla and a brightness to offset the richness of the dish.

Set aside pork shoulder (or butt) at room temperature for 1 to 1½ hours.

Preheat oven to 325°F.

Melt oil and 1 tablespoon butter in a large Dutch oven over medium-high heat. Generously season pork with salt and pepper. Add pork fat-side down and sear on one side for 3 to 4 minutes. Repeat with all sides. (The meat should be actively sizzling but not scorched. Adjust the heat if necessary.) Transfer pork to a platter, then remove fat from the pan drippings and discard.

Heat 2 tablespoons butter in the Dutch oven over medium heat. Add shallot and fennel and sauté for 10 minutes, until tender and caramelized. Add sage and cook for 1 minute. Stirring constantly, pour in wine and cook for 7 to 10 minutes, until reduced to a quarter of the original amount.

Add pork fat-side up, bay leaves, and salt and pepper. Pour in stock and bring to a simmer, then partially cover and cook in the oven for 1½ to 2 hours, until fork tender.

Uncover and cook for 15 minutes, until very fork tender. Remove from the oven.

Increase oven temperature to 350°F. Place hazelnuts on a baking sheet and toast for 7 to 10 minutes, until very golden. Set aside to cool, then finely chop.

Transfer pork to a platter. Using a slotted spoon, place fennel and shallot around it.

Strain sauce, then transfer back to the pan and bring to a simmer, skimming off any fat. Set aside. Whisk in 2 tablespoons cold butter and simmer for 30 seconds.

Ladle sauce over the pork, then garnish with hazelnuts, a few sage leaves, and finishing salt.

CHARRED CARROTS with

Anchovy Cream, Crisp Breadcrumbs, and Arugula CHEF: JOSH HENDERSON, HUXLEY WALLACE COLLECTIVE

8 large carrots
2 Tbsp olive oil (divided)
Salt and black pepper, to taste
4 anchovy fillets, finely chopped
1 Tbsp finely chopped shallot
¼ cup heavy cream
2 tsp lemon juice
1 slice rustic bread, cut into
   1-inch cubes (1 cup)
3 Tbsp salted butter, melted
Small handful of wild bunched
   arugula, for garnish

WINE PAIRING: Two Mountain Rosé

This dish is a superb starter on its own or perhaps as a side to something lighter, like oven-roasted halibut with white wine and herbs. It's the perfect dish for dining outside with friends in the warm weather. It's why this rosé works so well. Not only is it made for alfresco dining and summer foods, its red fruit and crisp acidity pairs nicely with grilled vegetables.

Preheat broiler to low heat.

   In a bowl, combine carrots, 1 tablespoon oil, and salt and pepper and toss. Place on a baking sheet and broil for 10 to 12 minutes, rotating occasionally for even caramelization, until tender. Increase broiler heat to high and cook for another 2 to 3 minutes, until carrots are charred. Set aside.

   Heat the remaining tablespoon oil in a skillet over medium heat. Add anchovies and shallot and sauté for 2 minutes. Add cream and lemon juice and simmer for 2 minutes. (If your sauce breaks, whisk in 1 tablespoon water or stock.)

   Preheat oven to 350°F.

   In a bowl, combine bread cubes and butter and toss. Place bread on a baking sheet and bake for 9 minutes, until well toasted. Set aside to cool, then pulse in a food processor until crumbled.

   Cut carrots diagonally on biases into large slices. Put a spoon of anchovy cream on the plate, then arrange carrots on top. Sprinkle breadcrumbs on top and garnish with arugula.

VA PIANO VINEYARDS

+

JUSTIN WYLIE

Va piano, meaning "go slowly" in Italian, is a cogent way of life that Justin Wylie adopted in 1995, while studying abroad in Florence, Italy. He was introduced to a culture passionate about food and wine, and he brought that same lifestyle to his hometown of Walla Walla when he returned a year later. "The term *va piano* reminded me to slow down after coming back to the States."

While Justin's enthusiasm for wine was sparked by his time abroad, it was his cousin, the late Eric Dunham, who exposed him to the world of winemaking and was a major inspiration for what Va Piano stands for today. He planted his first vines in 2000, around the same time Eric started Dunham Cellars. And today, Justin's wines are the unique expressions of the terroirs that abound on the leeward side of the Cascade Mountains, including their expansive estate-growing program in some of their vineyards.

Justin wants to make super balanced wine. "I like to produce wines that can be enjoyed mid-afternoon and late evening without the conundrum of it being light or too heavy." He hopes that his wines—whether an everyday wine like the Va Piano rosé or a small-lot-designated wine such as the Rosebud Vineyard Cabernet Sauvignon—will evoke emotional connections. In fact, it's one of the reasons why he built his winery at the bottom of a hill. "If you look around, there are no visual markers to let you know that you're in Walla Walla Valley. Your imagination can take you anywhere in the world." Including Italy.

LAMB CHOPS with Carrot
Mostarda, Kale, and Mushrooms

CHEF: JASON WILSON, FIRE & VINE HOSPITALITY

LAMB CHOPS

3 cloves garlic, finely chopped
2 sprigs rosemary, leaves only, finely chopped
2 Tbsp kosher salt
2 Tbsp extra-virgin olive oil
2 Tbsp balsamic vinegar
2 Tbsp whole-grain mustard
3 lbs lamb chops, thick cut and Frenched (ask your butcher)

MOSTARDA

½ lb carrots
1 Tbsp kosher salt, plus extra to taste
¼ tsp ground cinnamon
¼ tsp black pepper
¼ tsp ground cumin
¼ tsp ground coriander
2 Tbsp Dijon mustard
1 Tbsp prepared horseradish
Chicken stock (optional)

KALE AND MUSHROOMS

2 Tbsp olive oil
2 pints maitake or any wild mushrooms, sliced
2 cloves garlic, finely chopped
½ cup Syrah
1 Tbsp butter
Bunch of dino kale, finely chopped
Juice of 1 lemon
1 to 2 tsp kosher salt

WINE PAIRING: Va Piano Les Collines Vineyards Syrah

Lamb chops on the grill can be enjoyed any time of year. This dish is rich and tender and speaks only to quality ingredients, especially delicious vegetables. The Mediterranean-infused flavors pair well with the classic Syrah with its deep, dark fruit and dried herbs.

LAMB CHOPS In a large bowl, combine all ingredients except lamb chops and whisk. Add lamb and marinate for 30 minutes.

MOSTARDA Preheat oven to 375°F.

Place whole carrots on a baking sheet and roast for 30 minutes, until golden brown and tender.

In a food processor, combine carrots and the remaining ingredients except stock, if using, and purée until smooth and loose. If necessary, add a little chicken stock or water to thin out. Season with salt to taste.

KALE AND MUSHROOMS Heat oil in a skillet over high heat. Add mushrooms and cook for 4 minutes, until golden brown. Add garlic and cook for 3 minutes. Pour in wine and cook for another 3 minutes, until reduced by half and mushrooms are soft and tender. Set aside.

Melt butter in another skillet over medium heat. Add kale and cook for 10 minutes, until wilted. Add lemon juice and salt. Set aside.

ASSEMBLY Preheat grill to high heat. Add lamb chops and grill for 2 minutes per side per inch of thickness for medium-rare lamb chops. Transfer to a plate and set aside to rest for 5 minutes.

Spread a few dollops of mostarda on a large platter. Arrange mushrooms around the plate. Add kale, then arrange lamb on top. Serve immediately.

GRILLED PEACH SALAD
with Ricotta and Prosciutto

CHEF: JASON WILSON, FIRE & VINE HOSPITALITY

WINE PAIRING: Va Piano Sauvignon Blanc

With grilled peaches, creamy ricotta, and savory prosciutto, this salad is all about enjoying the seasons with a combination of winning flavors. Chef Jason Wilson pairs this with Va Piano's Sauvignon Blanc—its crisp minerality highlights the caramelized sweetness of grilled peaches and provides a clean contrast to the ricotta and Marcona almonds.

In a bowl, combine honey, wine, 1 tablespoon oil, 2 teaspoons salt, pepper, and chile. Add peaches, mix well, and set aside for 30 minutes to marinate.

In a small bowl, combine ricotta and 1 tablespoon oil. Set aside.

Preheat grill to high heat.

Grill peaches for 30 to 60 seconds on each side, until dark grill marks develop on the flesh side and light color can be seen on the skin. (Reserve marinade for later.) Transfer peaches to four plates.

Grill scallion tops and whites for 3 to 4 minutes on each side, until they have dark grill marks. (We want different textures and char marks.) Transfer scallions to a cutting board and chop them into large chunks.

To the reserved peach marinade, add the remaining 1 tablespoon oil, remaining 1 teaspoon salt, and scallions.

On a serving platter or individual plates, arrange arugula, peaches, ricotta mixture, herbs, prosciutto, and almonds. Drizzle scallion vinaigrette on top and season with salt.

2 Tbsp honey
1½ Tbsp Va Piano Sauvignon Blanc
3 Tbsp extra-virgin olive oil (divided)
3 tsp kosher or sea salt (divided), plus extra for finishing
1 tsp black pepper
1 tsp finely chopped Fresno chile
4 peaches, skin on, pitted, and cut into large wedges
⅔ cup ricotta
Bunch of scallions, trimmed and tops separated from whites
2 cups arugula
10 leaves mint, torn
5 leaves basil, torn
8 thinly sliced prosciutto
2 Tbsp Marcona almonds

W.T. VINTNERS

+

JEFF LINDSAY-THORSEN

Located in Woodinville's warehouse district, W.T. Vintners crafts terroir-driven wines, highlighting aromas, flavors, and nuances of the region. Their 2016 Les Collines Vineyard Damavian Blocks Syrah was named a Top 100 Wine by *Wine & Spirits* in 2019, the same year the magazine included W.T. Vintners as one of their Top 100 Wineries in the world. The 2015 Boushey Vineyard Syrah was chosen by *Seattle Met* as one of the 30 Most Exciting Wines in Washington in 2018, and *Seattle Magazine* named W.T. Vintners as Best Emerging Winery in 2017—all thanks to winemaker Jeff Lindsay-Thorsen (JLT).

While working at the original Lampreia restaurant in Seattle, JLT was introduced to two wines by a customer: a 1990 Domaine de la Romanée-Conti Echezeaux and a Henri Jayer Echezeaux. It was a life-altering experience that inspired him to change his course and make wines. With the help of his friend and future business partner, George White, they began experimenting with two barrels of Syrah. W.T. Vintners' first commercial vintage was produced in 2011.

Named a "Top 40 under 40" tastemaker by *Wine Enthusiast* magazine in 2018, JLT aspires to produce wines with tempered fruit. In a region renowned for fruity wines, his team coaxes out savory and earthy notes from the wines by allowing the voice of the vineyard to speak louder. "When you bring exceptional grapes into the cellar, it's my duty to fulfill their potential."

Sometimes a great bottle of wine can be so metamorphic, it will alter the career path of those who consume it.

> *Heirloom Tomato and Nectarine Salad with Squash Blossom Fritti* | *p. 216*

HEIRLOOM TOMATO AND NECTARINE SALAD with Squash

Blossom Fritti CHEF: HOLLY SMITH, CAFE JUANITA

Pictured p. 215

SERVES 5 TO 6

WINE PAIRING: W.T. Vintners Grüner Veltliner

This is chef Holly Smith's favorite summer salad. The flavors of nectarines and tomatoes are great together, and the hit of anchovy sauce (Colatura di Alici) brings them together. You want to cook squash blossoms soon after purchasing to maximize their freshness. When working with the batter, you'll need to whisk it continuously to prevent it from turning solid. Stir vigorously each time before coating the blossoms.

To accompany a dish this delicate, you need a light, acid-driven wine with spicy herbs and stone-fruit aromas. W.T. Vintners' Grüner Veltliner is a medium-bodied wine with bright acidity and a fresh, herbaceous character to complement this dish.

HEIRLOOM TOMATO AND NECTARINE SALAD Place shallot in a shallow bowl and drizzle over the Colatura di Alici (or regular fish sauce). Set aside for at least 20 minutes and up to 1½ hours, until fully macerated. To retain texture, drain macerated shallot and store in the refrigerator.

In a shallow bowl, combine tomatoes and nectarines (or peaches) and gently toss. Scatter half the shallot liberally over the fruit. Drizzle with oil, season with salt, and toss. The fruit will be sitting in a flavorful "soup" at this point.

AVOCADO MASH Mash avocado with fork. Season to taste with salt, cayenne, and lime juice. Do not make it as acidic as guacamole—this should be a fruity mash. Set aside until needed.

HEIRLOOM TOMATO AND NECTARINE SALAD

2 shallots, thinly sliced on a mandoline
¼ cup Colatura di Alici or Vietnamese fish sauce
4 ripe heirloom tomatoes, cored and cut into thick wedges
4 nectarines or peaches, pitted and cut into thick wedges
5 Tbsp good-quality fruity extra-virgin olive oil
Kosher salt, to taste

AVOCADO MASH

1 large ripe avocado
Kosher salt, to taste
Cayenne pepper, to taste
Lime juice, to taste

SQUASH BLOSSOM FRITTI

1⅓ cups rice flour
¾ cup + 1 Tbsp cornstarch
½ tsp baking powder
¼ tsp kosher salt, plus extra
  to taste
1½ cups vodka or sparkling
  or plain water
4 cups pure olive oil or canola oil,
  for deep-frying
10 to 12 fresh squash blossoms

SQUASH BLOSSOM FRITTI In a large bowl, combine flour, cornstarch, baking powder, salt, vodka (or sparkling or plain water), and ⅓ cup water. Using a whisk, mix well.

Heat oil in a deep fryer or deep saucepan until it reaches 325°F. Trim blossoms of the green stem and any hard ends. Dredge blossoms in batter, mixing the batter before you dredge each blossom (to prevent it from solidifying), and shake off any excess. Carefully lower blossoms in the hot oil, working in batches to avoid overcrowding. Deep-fry until the blossoms turn over in the oil and are lightly golden and crispy, about 2 minutes per side. Using a slotted spoon or metal spatula, carefully transfer blossoms to a paper-towel-lined plate, placing the open end down to drain any trapped oil. Season with salt.

ASSEMBLY To serve, place 2 heaping tablespoons of avocado mash on the bottom of a shallow bowl. Add tomato and nectarine salad on top and evenly distribute the remaining shallot. Add ¼ to ½ cup nectarine "soup" to the base (avoid pouring it over the avocado mash). Arrange blossoms on top, then serve immediately.

MUSCOVY DUCK BREAST
with Bing Cherries, Fennel Crema, Walla Walla Salad Onions, and Salsa Piccante

CHEF: HOLLY SMITH, CAFE JUANITA

WINE PAIRING: W.T. Vintners Boushey Vineyard Syrah

Renowned for its lean, tender meat, succulent Muscovy duck breast is served with dark bing cherries, sweet Walla Walla onions, and fresh local herbs—this is essentially Washington on a plate.

The W.T. Vintners' alluring Boushey Syrah has notes of herbs, cherry, olive, and black pepper. With both fruit and savory flavors to intrigue, it is the perfect complement to the dish.

SALSA PICCANTE Combine herbs and garlic and mix well. Season with chili oil, olive oil, lemon zest, and salt to taste. Set aside for at least 30 minutes to 2 hours. Add lemon juice. Taste, adjusting the seasoning if needed.

FENNEL CREMA Preheat oven to 350°F.

Place the fennel, vermouth and 6 tablespoons filtered water to a 2-inch baking dish. Season with salt and cover tightly with aluminum foil. Bake for 30 minutes, until fennel is very tender.

Drain fennel of liquid, reserving 2 tablespoons. Put fennel in a high-speed blender and blend until smooth, adding a little reserved liquid if necessary. Season with salt, cayenne, and lemon juice. Keep warm.

WALLA WALLA SALAD ONIONS Preheat oven to 400°F.

In a bowl, combine onion and oil and season with salt. Add herbs, if using.

Place on a parchment-lined baking sheet and bake for 12 to 16 minutes, until tender. Keep warm.

SYRAH BING CHERRY SAUCE Put herbs in an herb sachet.

Heat oil in a skillet over medium-low heat. Add shallot and cook for 2 to 3 minutes.

Pour in wine, then add herb sachet. Cook for 5 minutes, until reduced by a third. Add stock and cook over medium heat for another 10 to 15 minutes, until the sauce coats the back of a spoon. Pass mixture through a fine-mesh strainer. Season with salt. Keep warm. (Cherries will be added right before serving.)

SALSA PICCANTE
½ bunch parsley, chopped
4 sprigs mint, leaves only, chopped
2 sprigs tarragon, leaves only, chopped
1 clove garlic, chopped
Italian chili oil, such as Calabrian, to taste
2 Tbsp extra-virgin olive oil
Grated zest and juice of ½ lemon
Kosher salt

FENNEL CREMA
2 large bulbs fennel, cored and cut into wedges
4 fl oz dry white vermouth (preferably Dolin Vermouth de Chambéry)
Pinch of kosher salt, plus extra for seasoning
Small pinch of cayenne pepper
Juice of ½ lemon

WALLA WALLA SALAD ONIONS
4 sweet onions, such as Walla Walla or Vidalia, peeled and quartered, root end intact
3 Tbsp extra-virgin olive oil
Kosher salt
Sprigs of rosemary and thyme (optional)

SYRAH BING CHERRY SAUCE
4 sprigs thyme
Sprig of rosemary
1 bay leaf
1 Tbsp extra-virgin olive oil
1 shallot, thinly sliced
2 cups W.T. Vintners Syrah
3 cups best-quality chicken stock, skimmed
Salt, to taste

MUSCOVY DUCK BREAST

4 to 6 Muscovy duck breasts,
trimmed of excess fat

2 bunches thyme or summer
savory

Kosher salt and black pepper,
to taste

ASSEMBLY

1 tsp butter (optional)

1 cup bing cherries, pitted and
halved, room temperature

MUSCOVY DUCK BREAST Using a sharp knife, score duck skin in a crosshatch pattern, taking care not to cut into meat. Remove leaves from half the thyme (or summer savory) and sprinkle them on the bottom of a shallow container. Add duck breasts skin-side up and place remaining bunch of thyme on top. Refrigerate, uncovered, for at least 6 hours and up to 24 hours. Remove thyme sprigs, reserving some for when cooking the duck.

Pre-heat a large cast-iron skillet over medium-high heat. Generously season the skin with salt and pepper. Cook duck, skin-side down, until duck releases most of its fat and the skin is well caramelized.

Add thyme and using a large spoon, baste meat with hot duck fat. If needed, pour out excess fat, leaving enough for basting. Cook for 8 to 10 minutes, or until skin is well rendered and crisp. Turn over duck breasts, skin-side up, and cook for 1 minute or until you reach your desired doneness (130°F for medium-rare). Turn off heat, transfer duck to a cooling rack in a warm location, and set aside for 10 minutes to rest.

ASSEMBLY Add butter or any duck drippings into cherry sauce and stir. Add cherries.

To serve, place a dollop of fennel crema on plate and place the onions alongside the crema. Drizzle salsa piccante over the onions. Slice the duck breast and place half on the crema and half on the onions. Finish by saucing the plate with the cherry sauce, making sure everyone receives a few cherries.

METRIC CONVERSION CHART

VOLUME

Imperial	Metric
⅛ tsp	0.5 ml
¼ tsp	1 ml
½ tsp	2.5 ml
¾ tsp	4 ml
1 tsp	5 ml
½ Tbsp	8 ml
1 Tbsp	15 ml
1½ Tbsp	23 ml
2 Tbsp	30 ml
¼ cup	60 ml
⅓ cup	80 ml
½ cup	125 ml
⅔ cup	165 ml
¾ cup	185 ml
1 cup	250 ml
1¼ cups	310 ml
1⅓ cups	330 ml
1½ cups	375 ml
1⅔ cups	415 ml
1¾ cups	435 ml
2 cups	500 ml
2¼ cups	560 ml
2⅓ cups	580 ml
2½ cups	625 ml
2¾ cups	690 ml
3 cups	750 ml
4 cups / 1 quart	1 L
5 cups	1.25 L
6 cups	1.5 L
7 cups	1.75 L
8 cups / 2 quarts	2 L

WEIGHT

Imperial	Metric
½ oz	15 g
1 oz	30 g
2 oz	60 g
3 oz	85 g
4 oz (¼ lb)	115 g
5 oz	140 g
6 oz	170 g
7 oz	200 g
8 oz (½ lb)	225 g
9 oz	255 g
10 oz	285 g
11 oz	310 g
12 oz (¾ lb)	340 g
13 oz	370 g
14 oz	400 g
15 oz	425 g
16 oz (1 lb)	450 g
1¼ lbs	570 g
1½ lbs	670 g
2 lbs	900 g
3 lbs	1.4 kg
4 lbs	1.8 kg
5 lbs	2.3 kg
6 lbs	2.7 kg

LIQUID MEASURES (for alcohol)

Imperial	Metric
1 fl oz	30 ml
2 fl oz	60 ml
3 fl oz	90 ml
4 fl oz	120 ml

CANS AND JARS

Imperial	Metric
14 oz	398 ml
28 oz	796 ml

LINEAR

Imperial	Metric
⅛ inch	3 mm
¼ inch	6 mm
½ inch	12 mm
¾ inch	2 cm
1 inch	2.5 cm
1¼ inches	3 cm
1½ inches	3.5 cm
1¾ inches	4.5 cm
2 inches	5 cm
2½ inches	6.5 cm
3 inches	7.5 cm
4 inches	10 cm
5 inches	12.5 cm
6 inches	15 cm
7 inches	18 cm
8 inches	20 cm
9 inches	23 cm
10 inches	25 cm
11 inches	28 cm
12 inches (1 foot)	30 cm
13 inches	33 cm
18 inches	46 cm

TEMPERATURE

Imperial	Metric
90°F	32°C
120°F	49°C
125°F	52°C
130°F	54°C
135°F	57°C
140°F	60°C
145°F	63°C
150°F	66°C
155°F	68°C
160°F	71°C
165°F	74°C
170°F	77°C
175°F	80°C
180°F	82°C
185°F	85°C
190°F	88°C
195°F	91°C
200°F	93°C
225°F	107°C
250°F	121°C
275°F	135°C
300°F	149°C
325°F	163°C
350°F	177°C
360°F	182°C
375°F	191°C

OVEN TEMPERATURE

Imperial	Metric
200°F	95°C
250°F	120°C
275°F	135°C
300°F	150°C
325°F	160°C
350°F	180°C
375°F	190°C
400°F	200°C
425°F	220°C
450°F	230°C

BAKING PANS

Imperial	Metric
5- × 9-inch loaf pan	2 L loaf pan
9- × 13-inch cake pan	4 L cake pan
13- × 18-inch baking sheet	33 × 46 cm baking sheet

ACKNOWLEDGMENTS

I've had the privilege to work with some of the most talented people in wine, food, and publishing on this project. And without getting too maudlin (yes, some wine is involved in the writing of this sentiment), this book would not be the same without each and every one of them.

First, thank you to the team at Figure 1—Michelle Meade, Chris Labonté, Richard Nadeau, Lara Smith, Mark Redmayne, and Michelle Young—who've been the best support team an author could ask for. Thank you to copy editor Grace Yaginuma who spent long days and nights reviewing the copy to ensure this book was the best version of itself. Proofreader Renate Preuss was the final step in the editing process. To them, I am so grateful.

I'd like to extend my gratitude to the delightful photographer Charity Burggraaf, who is a powerhouse behind the camera; photo assistant Amy Johnson for managing everything so smoothly behind the scenes; and creative director Jessica Sullivan, who delivered a skilled and precise vision for the layout.

A special thank-you to the chefs who created recipes for this book. It was not an easy task, and I am incredibly appreciative of their participation. I also owe my gratitude to recipe tester Justin Khanna, who had the daunting task of re-creating all of the recipes, and who was available around the clock to answer the most meticulous questions. Food stylist Nathan Carrabba turned those recipes into visual masterpieces with the help of assistant CeiCei Shue.

The gorgeousness of the food was accentuated by handcrafted tableware courtesy of Goose Creek Mercantile, Beau Rush, and Natasha Alphonse Ceramics Studio.

I also have a list of people to thank for sharing their wine knowledge and connections with me, including Ryan Pennington, who has been my go-to encyclopedia of Washington wine for years; Heather Bradshaw and Averyl Dunn from the Washington State Wine Commission; Kristin Ackerman Bacon and Erin James from *Sip* magazine; and Annie Sullivan.

The generosity of Kyle MacLachlan who took time out of his demanding schedule to write the foreword of this book, which celebrates his fellow Washington winemakers and the farm-to-table cuisine he grew up on, is a true gift which I am forever thankful for.

And finally, the winemakers. It was an incredible honor to hear their anecdotes and to learn about their wines. Their commitment to this book and their trust in me to accurately portray their stories leave me humbled. I thank all of them for their patience and dedication to this process. I hope to be sharing a bottle and a meal with them soon.

INDEX

JULIEN PERRY has been a food and lifestyle writer and editor for more than twenty years, and has worked as a food editor for *Seattle Weekly*, *Seattle Business Magazine*, *Eater Seattle*, and *Seattle Magazine*. Her work has also been featured in *Food & Wine* and on the Food Network. An alumnus of the University of Washington Department of Communications and the Seattle Art Institute Baking and Pastry program, she cofounded the One Night Only Project—a roving dinner series that partners with the city's food and beverage powerhouses—and Chefodex, a chef-for-hire service featuring a roster of Seattle's foremost culinary talent.

OTHER BOOKS BY AUTHOR: